Carpets of Central Persia
With special reference to rugs of Kirman

May H. Beattie

Mappin Art Gallery, Sheffield
10 April–19 May 1976

City Museum and Art Gallery, Birmingham
4 June–11 July 1976

D1451888

World of Islam Festival Publishing Company Ltd

First published 1976
ISBN 0 905035 16 X cased
ISBN 0 905035 17 8 paper

Published and produced by the World of Islam Festival Publishing Company Ltd.

Designed by Colin Larkin
Edited by Halina Tunikowska
Set in 10/11 pt Monophoto Plantin 110
Printed on 115 gsm Blade coated cartridge

Colour origination: Westerham Press
Filmset by Westerham Press and printed in England by Westerham Press Ltd., Westerham, Kent.

Front cover photograph:
Arabesque, animal and sickle-leaf border design (no. 24).

Back cover photograph:
Detail of multiple-medallion carpet (no. 7 and Colour Plate 4).

Contents

List of Lenders

Baghdad, Iraq Museum: 44

Baltimore, Baltimore Museum of Art: 43, 51

Berlin, Museum für Islamische Kunst Stiftung Preussischer Kulturbesitz: 34

Boston, Boston Museum of Fine Arts: 26, 40, 60

Cambridge, Mass., Fogg Art Museum, Harvard University: 47

Düsseldorf, Kunstmuseum: 55

Frankfurt-am-Main, Museum für Kunsthandwerk: 10

Glasgow, Burrell Collection, Glasgow Art Gallery and Museum: 1,
18, 28, 36, 37, 39, 45, 57, 61

Kettering, His Grace The Duke of Buccleuch and Queensberry,
VRD: 5a, 7

London, John Hewett: 4, 48; Keir Collection: 31, 62; Victoria and
Albert Museum: 14, 19, 35, 38, 52

Lugano, Thyssen-Bornemisza Collection: 2, 8

Lyons, Musée des Tissus: 24, 41, 58

Madrid, Instituto Valencia de Don Juan: 1b

Munich, Firma Bernheimer: 9, 11, 29, 32; Staatliches Museum für
Völkerkunde: 17, 23, 25

New York, Metropolitan Museum of Art: 30, 42

Paris, Musée du Louvre: 5, 6, 21, 27, 54

Washington, Textile Museum: 3, 12, 13, 16, 20, 22, 33, 46, 49, 50, 56;
Corcoran Gallery of Art: 15

Williamsburg, Colonial Williamsburg Foundation: 53

Foreword

The present exhibition is the fruit of many months of planning and hard work since Dr May Beattie first outlined the idea to us in 1974. Her deep knowledge of the subject, dedication and single-mindedness in pursuing often difficult and obscure trails and references have paid off handsomely as witnessed by the many delights now gathered together. In addition to selecting the exhibits, Dr Beattie has also written the introduction and notes for this catalogue, which we are confident will be not only a fascinating accompaniment to the exhibition, but an essential addition to the bookshelves of all with an interest in Islamic art.

The opportunity to make direct comparisons between examples normally scattered throughout the world is one of the most valuable aspects of the exhibition, and our sincere thanks are due to all the owners, both here and abroad, who have generously lent their precious possessions, whether carpets, rugs or fragments, to enable us to illustrate our theme so fully.

We are deeply grateful to the Festival of Islam committee who have throughout generously supported this project, one of two provincial exhibitions within the overall Festival theme for 1976.

Considerable help and advice has been forthcoming from the many museums, embassy staffs and private individuals whom we have consulted and our sincere thanks are offered; in particular to the staff of the Textile Museum, Washington D.C., who readily responded to our requests for information and advice on several occasions. Finally, a word of thanks to Mrs Marian Pierce and her colleagues who have laboured for many months on less spectacular, but highly important, aspects of the exhibition.

Frank Constantine
Director, Sheffield City Art Galleries
January 1976

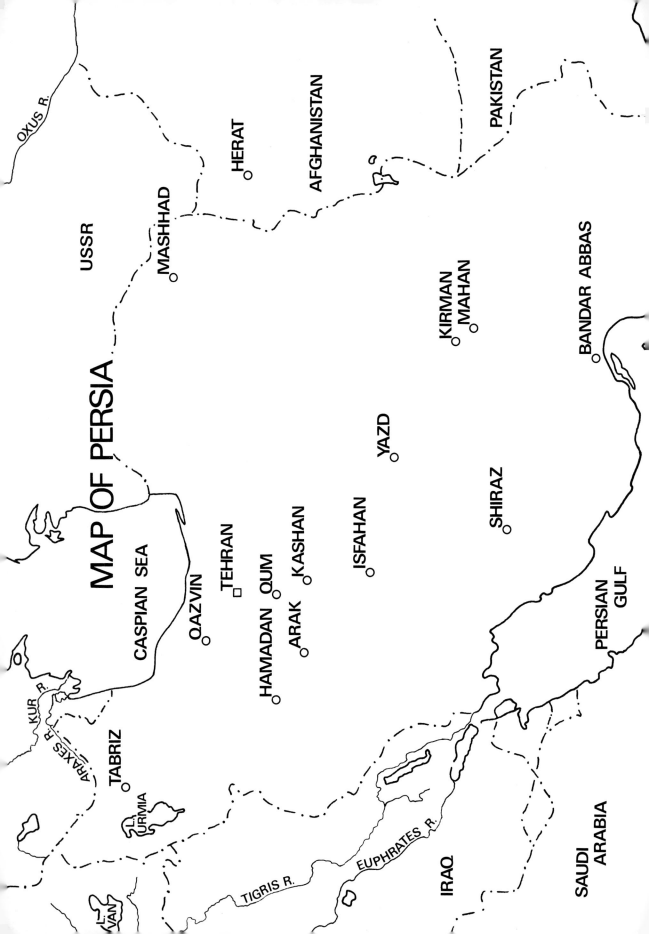

Introduction

From time to time writers of classical antiquity mention carpets, but for many centuries the term was also applied to tapestries and other textiles constructed quite differently from the modern knotted carpet. It is therefore uncertain which, if any, of the early observations really referred to pile rugs as we now know them. Fragments from the early centuries of the first millennium have occasionally been excavated in countries of the Middle East and Central Asia, and a high proportion of the weaves differ from those in use today. It is only in recent years that these atypical weaves have come to be regarded as an aspect of the Oriental rug which must be studied if a complete picture of the subject is to be obtained.

The whole situation changed in 1949 when a pile carpet of typical weave,[1] was excavated near the village of Pazyryk in the Altai mountains of Siberia. According to carbon dating and dendrochronology, objects found in the burial mound dated from about the fourth century B.C.,[2] perhaps only a few decades before Alexander the Great campaigned in the Middle East. The stylized lotus-and-bud pattern of the field is the same as that of designs carved in low relief on some of the stone slabs which were found at the portals of Assyrian halls, and therefore dates from before the fall of Nineveh in 612 B.C. when the Medes and Babylonians overthrew the Assyrian Empire. To judge from the quality of the design, the dyes and the workmanship of the Pazyryk carpet, the craft of the carpet weaver must have been in full swing many centuries before Cyrus the Great (559–530 B.C.) founded the Persian Empire. More than a thousand years later the Prophet Muḥammad established the religion which united people of many races as the World of Islam. Carpets are usually classified as one of the arts of Islam, although we now know that they were being woven long before the death of the Prophet in A.D. 632. As a result of subsequent conquests Muslim influence soon extended from Spain to China, with, eventually and inevitably, an exchange of decorative motifs and techniques throughout that vast area.

Evidence abounds for the weaving of pile carpets following the westward movements of the Turks and the Mongols in the eleventh and thirteenth centuries, both of whom eventually adopted the Muslim faith; and the rapid methods of knotting used by their weavers no doubt did much to displace the more primitive techniques which were still current in the Mediterranean regions. Carpets became increasingly familiar in western Europe from the period of the Crusades onwards. They were depicted in paintings by artists

[1] Rudenko p. 13

[2] Jettmar p. 135

who appreciated the effect of bold colourful designs beneath the feet of a Madonna or across a burgher's table. The majority were in the angular Anatolian style, whereas Persian rugs, more often in curvilinear designs, were not reproduced to the same extent in western paintings. Indeed the importation of Persian carpets seems to have been small until trade with that country got under way in the seventeenth century.

Our scant knowledge of Persian carpets from the Mongol period until the rise of the Safavid dynasty in the early sixteenth century is also derived from paintings, but, in this case, from Persian miniatures in which the brilliant colours and fine details of the tiles and costumes and gardens are matched by the equally brilliant colours of the carpets. The usual carpet designs depicted in miniatures prior to the rise of the Safavid dynasty in 1502 are repetitive, largely rectilinear, field patterns with small curvilinear details, often enclosed in 'Kufic' borders, a type of decoration derived from an early angular form of Arabic script. With the coming of the Mongols, rug designs, just as much as those of the other arts of Islam, must have reflected the graceful Far Eastern styles. In a miniature painting from about the time of the break-up of the Mongol Empire in Persia in the second quarter of the fourteenth century, a rug is depicted with a curvilinear field pattern in which two birds, in floral surroundings, face each other across a floral motif,[3] and another of A.D. 1445 has what may be the earliest centralized design so far known.[4] In the latter, endless knots link three medallions and well-drawn floral scrolls fill the field, but the borders of both these rugs are of the rectilinear 'Kufic' type which is so often depicted in miniatures of the Timurid period. It is not known to what extent such designs in miniatures represent actual carpets because, apart from occasional small fragments, no Persian pile carpets are known to have survived from the fourteenth and fifteenth centuries, but it seems reasonable to suppose that curvilinear floral and centralized designs, some with animate forms, persisted as an undercurrent in Persian carpet design even when the repetitive, often rather angular, Timurid style was at its height.

The renewed influence of Far Eastern design became obvious in the Safavid period (1502–1732) when dragons and *ch'i-lins* and other mythological creatures – identified by flame-like emanations rising from shoulder and hip, 'clouds' in various styles including the small coiled forms, lotuses and a great variety of other exotic motifs appeared in the designs of Persian carpets. In the seventeenth century the widespread use of carpets in the East and the gaiety of their colours immediately impressed western travellers. Naturally, in Persia, the most striking were the glittering confections of silk and gold (Plate 12 and no. 5a) which were 'the peculiar Manufacture of the Country'.[5] At one time they were referred to as 'Polish' carpets in the mistaken belief that they were made in Poland. The confusion which resulted is only gradually being dispelled and the term 'Polonaise', suggestive of the dance and of music and thus well suited to the rich materials and rhythmic designs of this type, makes an appropriate name.

Documents, written by travellers, missionaries and historians, both Oriental and European, and inventories and other records, provide evidence for the weaving of carpets in different parts of

[3] Ipsiroglu Pl. 23

[4] Ettinghausen 1971 No. 41

[5] Fryer II p. 248

Persia. There are many references, but in only a few instances can the comments on materials or designs be tied quite definitely to specific places. These, reinforced by a mass of less precise evidence, make it as certain as can now be that some surviving carpets were woven in places specified in documents.

Shāh 'Abbās I (1588–1629) established royal factories for the weaving of carpets[6] in widely separate centres including Kashan, Kirman and his capital Isfahan, all of which are situated on the vast highland of central Persia. Even in Isfahan in the early 1670s there were still thirty-two royal workshops for various products.[7] From the frequent references there is no doubt that enormous numbers of 'silk and gold' carpets were woven, notably in Kashan[8] and Isfahan.[9] Silk tapestries or kilims are also mentioned and several bearing the arms of the Polish King Sigismund III Wasa (1587–1632), who is known to have ordered carpets of silk and gold in Kashan[10] still exist. Chardin[11] provides the information that both silk and worsted 'Droguets' (druggets) were made in Yazd and Kirman, and Ovington[12] comments on the 'richest and fairest tapestries of all Persia' near Yazd.

In the sixteenth century carpets from Kirman and Joshagan as well as from Khuzistan and Sabzawar were imported into India.[13] Both the former were famous wool-producing centres, and, at the beginning of the seventeenth century, carpets of Kirman took second place only to those of Yazd.[14] In the second quarter of the century Tavernier[15] mentions woollen carpets, as well as those of silk, and of silk and gold, being woven in Isfahan in the palace workshops just off the Maidan.

Shāh 'Abbās himself was skilled in carpet weaving[16] and his interest in carpets, which for centuries had been important merchandise, the establishment of the factories and his own activities as a merchant – perhaps even the requirements for the furnishing of his palaces in the splendid new capital of Isfahan – must all have combined to stimulate the production of magnificent carpets in both silk and wool. It was during his reign that western merchant adventurers began to arrive in Persia and Persian carpets began to arrive in appreciable numbers in the West.

The materials used in the silk-pile carpets make them easily recognized among surviving rugs and we therefore know some of the designs which were used. Two groups of carpets referred to respectively as the Large and the Small Silk Carpets of Kashan (no. 5, Plate 3) and some of the silk kilims (nos. 6 and 8) usually assigned to Kashan often contain animals, although these are unknown in Polonaise carpets, but what the designs of the contemporary woollen-pile carpets from the same area or the silk and woollen kilims from Yazd and Kirman were like is unknown.

Pope[17] assigned the woollen-pile Vase carpets to Joshagan, probably the village some seventy-six miles north of Isfahan, the Sanguszko animal carpets to Kirman or possibly Yazd; Erdmann,[18] as already mentioned, contended that the latter were from Kashan, the former from Kirman. The one useful clue elicited so far from the literature[19] is the observation made by Engelbert Kaempfer in 1684 that the most splendid decoration of a reception hall in Isfahan consisted of Kirman carpets with animal designs, knotted of the finest wool. If this does not refer to animal carpets such as some of

[6] Mańkowski p. 2431 note 5

[7] Chardin II p. 18

[8] Florencio II p. 102
[9] Tavernier I pp. 397 589

[10] Mańkowski p. 2433, Erdmann 1938 p. 64
[11] III p. 120
[12] p. 375

[13] Abul Fazl I p. 55

[14] Teixeira p. 243 note 2
[15] I p. 589

[16] Florencio III p. 22

[17] Surv. p. 2357

[18] 1941 p. 189

[19] Spuhler 1968a p. 141

[20] p. 41

those in the present exhibition it is difficult to know to which famous carpets he refers.

The destruction of carpets down the centuries must undoubtedly have been enormous. Sir Thomas Arnold's comments[20] on the difficulties in the way of studying Islamic paintings and the sorry fate which must have befallen so many of them are almost equally applicable to carpets, and although the latter are of sturdier stuff than paintings, the rougher treatment to which they are normally subjected makes them extremely vulnerable. In exceptional cases beautiful rugs have survived almost intact from the sixteenth and seventeenth centuries, for it is natural that the finest are the most treasured, but, on the whole, the older the carpet, the greater will be the wear and tear. It follows, therefore, that evidence for early designs is more likely to be found among tattered remains than among the handsome, well-preserved carpets which museum and exhibition organizers understandably prefer to present to the public. One or two collectors, notably Wilhelm von Bode, Friedrich Sarre and F. R. Martin in Europe, and George Hewitt Myers and Denman Ross in the United States, interested themselves in fragments which were often small and apparently insignificant. In recent years with the increasing scarcity of old rugs, and with easier travel and rising interest in the subject as a whole, the whereabouts of these pieces and their importance as representatives of lost types or links in a chain of designs or just as parts of widely dispersed fragmentary carpets are rapidly becoming evident.

When carpets aroused the interest of collectors in the nineteenth century little was known of their origins and writers only went so far as to assign them to wide geographical areas such as Persia or India. With the publication of Martin's remarkable book in 1908 the situation changed. He had spent a considerable time in the Middle East and apparently made numerous enquiries in the bazaars as to the provenance of various carpet types. Up to then designs which he illustrated were apparently still unknown in Europe and much of what he wrote has been the foundation on which opinions of later writers were based. The information he obtained about some of the pieces which he collected was that they came from South Persian mosques and that they had reached Istanbul and centres further west only in the ten years before he wrote. A number of these historic fragments, or additional parts of the same carpets, are exhibited in Sheffield as well as other rugs which he illustrated in his book. Gradually carpets were grouped on the basis of design and materials but the inevitable use of monochrome photographs made comparisons of colours extremely difficult.

What seems to have been the first exhibition of antique rugs of one specific type was that held in 1930 in the Metropolitan Museum of Art in New York. Dr Dimand discussed twenty-seven of the lustrous silk Polonaise carpets in his catalogue. Until that time it had been customary, when exhibiting carpets, to select the best possible examples from different geographical areas and different periods. In 1940, apparently overlooking the 1930 exhibition, the Textile Museum in Washington decided that the time had come 'to divert attention from all-embracing surveys and descriptive cataloguings to specific studies of individual types'. Thirty-seven Caucasian

Dragon carpets were brought together. The monograph on the subject, which was envisaged at the time and which was obviously intended to contain an assessment of the observations drawn from a comparative study of the actual rugs, never materialized, and the slim catalogue with two illustrations and entries of a few lines is little more than a list of exhibits and owners.

In recent years the Textile Museum has mounted several splendid exhibitions of its own and other antique rugs, and museums and rug societies have brought together Kazaks, Turkomans and similar groups of later date. In 1969 the museum carried the specialized approach a step further with an exhibition devoted to kilims and a considerable variety of other flat weaves few of which predate the nineteenth century; but they were grouped according to the way in which they were woven, and the catalogue[21] is an invaluable aid to the study of such pieces.

[21] Landreau & Pickering

The Sheffield exhibition takes this objective approach somewhat further. It deals almost exclusively with a class of antique pile carpets selected because of the rather characteristic way in which they are woven. The rugs are then subdivided and grouped by design, and motifs common to two or more groups often show the close relationship which exists between them.

For the purposes of this catalogue the weave will be referred to as the 'vase'-technique because this was the method of weaving the famous group of Vase carpets; and the carpets, provisionally, and for want of a better term, will be referred to as 'Vase'-technique carpets. A vase, with or without a bracket, was the motif in the lattice designs (p. 26) which caught the attention of early writers and gave rise to the name 'Vase carpets', regardless of the fact that some of the designs contain no vases, that other rugs structurally similar but different in design do, and that yet others quite different in structure, style and colouring also have vases. When the last are discussed without explanations along with 'Vase'-technique rugs, one can only sympathize with the reader. The term stuck and its indiscriminate application to various groups of designs in rugs woven in the 'vase'-technique is an exasperating waste of time as the tedious checking of references to pieces illustrated in other publications soon shows.

The structure of intact carpets woven in the 'vase'-technique is particularly difficult to determine because of the closely compressed weave, and without ample time the satisfactory examination of a carpet at several different points becomes impossible.

[22] Beattie 1961 p. 6

A study of fragments in the Burrell Collection[22] in Glasgow provided much useful information. Cut and worn edges and abraded surfaces make examination easier and it soon appeared that rugs in sickle-leaf, arabesque, lattice and medallion designs, and even the famous Wagner Garden carpet (Plate 1, no. 1) were structurally alike. Subsequently a whole series of famous carpets and less well-known fragments was examined and, as far as can be judged from widely distributed pieces studied at intervals of some time, a similar weave with occasionally minor variations is common to all of them. The designs of course included the Vase carpets, but what was surprising at the time was to find that carpets with pictorial or scenic designs such as the Williams medallion fragment (no. 63) in Philadelphia, the Stieglitz half carpet (no. 1a) in the Hermitage Museum in Leningrad, as well as certain carpets of the well known Sanguszko group (nos. 2 and 3) and the animal fragments in Munich (no. 11) and Frankfurt (no. 10) were all woven in the same way.

Although the importance of recording how a carpet was woven was recognized as early as 1892 in the Vienna Book there were hardly enough rugs of one type in any one exhibition to make a comparison of the findings worth while. Furthermore, individual opinions regarding the nature of materials and structure differed widely, and even in some of the most valuable of the early books discrepancies in the technical findings of rugs now known to be woven in the 'vase'-technique would have made any attempt to collate the early records of little value.

The title *Carpets of Central Persia* has been chosen for the exhibition in order to present as unbiased a view as possible. Here 'Central Persia' is defined as that plateau area bounded to the north by the Caucasian and Alburz range, to the south and west by the Zagros range and to the east by the desert – an area thus encompassing a vast stretch of territory from Tabriz to Kirman. It includes centres with a tradition of carpet weaving long before the sixteenth and seventeenth centuries. The collected opinions of nearly a century of scholars place most of the carpets in the exhibition in this very area, but opinions differ as to where exactly certain rugs come from.

Since one of the purposes of the exhibition is to show as many designs as possible of rugs woven in the 'vase'-technique, condition has not been a prime consideration in selection. Another purpose is to determine whether a weave, which appears to be of one type when recorded on paper in different places, is in fact the same when comparisons are made with the rugs side by side. It may emerge that some of the rugs believed to be in the 'vase'-technique cannot be so classified. Whether the exhibition will help to solve some of the vexed questions of provenance and the area of distribution of this particular type of weave remains to be seen.

The question of provenance is best left until after the exhibition. The most important problem is whether or not the so-called Sanguszko carpets (see p. 32) come from the same area as the 'Vase'-technique rugs, as the weave suggests, or from Kashan as Erdmann[23] suggests. He bases his arguments for a Kashan origin on a series of design comparisons:

1. The borders of the Taylor, Madrid (no. 1b) and Lyons (no. 66) carpets with that of the Doistau kilim (no. 6).
2. The dragon and phoenix combat in the Madrid and Sanguszko carpets with those in the Pādishāh kilims in Berlin,[24] Washington[25] and Copenhagen.[26]
3. The spandrel filling of the Sanguszko carpet with that of the Hunting kilim in Munich.[27]
4. The figure-filled cartouche mosaic of the Buccleuch carpet (no. 7, Plate 4) with the similar arrangement in the Figdor kilim (no. 8) and the use of larger animals in the cartouche of the latter with those in the Pādishāh kilims and the Woods Bliss kilim.[28]
5. The spotted deer in the Madrid carpet (no. 1b) with those in the Munich Hunting kilim, or the scenes in the pictorially arranged design of the Paris carpet (no. 68) with those in the spandrels of the Doistau kilim (no. 6).

[23] 1941 p. 170

[24] Sarre & Trenkwald II Pl. 45
[25] Surv. Pl. 1267
[26] Martin Fig. 158

[27] Surv. Pl. 1264

[28] Sarre & Trenkwald II Pl. 46

Erdmann also mentions colour comparisons, but the difficulties of assessing colours when the rugs are not side by side is obvious.

The introduction of a number of rugs of quite different types makes possible, in a limited way, further comparisons of materials, structure, colour and style.

It is hoped that those with a profound knowledge of Islamic art will take the opportunity of studying the rugs, particularly those characteristics which can never satisfactorily be assessed from photographs, and that, in due course, they will publish their conclusions, or at least discuss them with the organizers of the exhibition. Suggestions for a more appropriate name for this class of carpets would be most welcome.

Technical Information

Weave

The structure and 'handle' of 'Vase'-technique rugs differ considerably from woollen rugs assigned to Northwest or East Persia. As in any type of handwork some variation from the norm is to be expected. The weavers use firmly plied Z4S ivory cotton for the *warps*, but at times one finds light blue or shades of pink.

There are three passes of *weft* after each row of knots. The first and third are of Z2Sw wool, tightly stretched between the closely laid warps, which are thus divided into a definite upper and lower plane, the two being held together by a fine second weft. Much of the woollen weft yarn may be in shades of ash, brindle (mixed fibres in natural colours) and brown, but an unusual feature is the use of varying amounts of coloured yarn such as is found in the pile. The introduction of these coloured wefts seems to be quite haphazard as though to utilize available oddments of wool. The use of yarns and dyes in the fine second wefts is somewhat more regular than in the case of the first and third woollen ones. Silk, in all or some of the second wefts, appears in rugs of the best quality but a Z2Sw cotton weft is much more usual. At times one strand may be silk, the other cotton. There may even be a few rows of fine wool and this yarn predominates in the second wefts in two rugs usually classified with the Sanguszko group, no. 1b and no. 64. Regrettably these two carpets are not available for the exhibition. Apart from natural light cotton, preference goes to pink and blue with occasionally other shades, even orange, but deep red is most usual in silk.

On worn surfaces commencing disintegration of the second weft is shown by patches of transverse lines, really slight ridges, which result from release of the warps when the second weft breaks. Massive breakdown of the second wefts in succeeding rows releases lengths of warps which lie in conspicuous and rather characteristic parallel lines on the surfaces of the rug, although it is still held together by the sturdy first and third woollen wefts. There is little doubt that while the fine second weft allows dense packing of the pile, in the long run it is an inherent weakness in structure.

Transverse lines similar to those just mentioned, but passing right across the rug, occur at irregular intervals of an inch or two in some rugs. Ellis[1] interpreted these as the absence of the second weft, but following further studies[2] believes the effect is due to a single heavy weft comparable to those found in certain Caucasian carpets. In view of the close relationships of designs in the two areas this would hardly be surprising. The point needs further study.

The *pile* of the 'Vase'-technique rugs is of Z2Sw wool and is

[1] 1968 p. 26
[2] Washington 1975 p. 26

attached by means of the asymmetrical *knot* open at the left. In many rugs the *count* runs about 14 × 15 knots per linear inch. Neither silk pile nor metal brocading has been found in rugs of characteristic weave. The former is surprising as the use of silk in some second wefts shows that it was available. Silk-pile rugs from the same area may once have existed but none is recognized. Identification would have to be made by colour and style.

A heavy woollen *backshag* – the equivalent of a built-in underfelt – characterizes some of the rugs in the large-leaf lattice design (p. 27) and among the knotted pile carpets of Persia of the classical period this is the only group known to have this feature. The shag, originally looped and several inches in length, is knotted to the back of the lower plane of warps; and those who sat upon such rugs no doubt enjoyed the additional warmth and resilience. Most of the shag is a rich, yellowish wool but in some fragments blue and red stripes an inch or two in width add colour at the sides.

Colour

In many great Persian carpets primary colours are used for the field. It is unusual to find secondary colours used to the same extent if at all. The designs of the 'Vase'-technique rugs stand out not only against dark blue and red but also against a brighter blue (no. 32), a dusky pink (no. 24), and yellow, both pale (no. 3) and a rich ochre (no. 58). A rusty orange background appears in a directional flowering-plant design (no. 14); rust in a small fragment of a lattice pattern (no. 43), and the field of a three-plane lattice carpet (no. 44) in Baghdad, now in pieces, has a variegated green field. The dark purple, which might be regarded as an aberrant indigo in the border of no. 28, is quite definite in the field of nos. 41 and 25. Colours may be pale or dark, warm or cold, and brilliant tomato red occurs along with touches of pale violet. A curious uneven chestnut colour slightly streaked with a dull blue seems to result from the use of red and blue on natural, varicoloured brown yarn. Shades of ivory (no. 2) and dark brown are less common, although the well-known erosive effect which results from dyeing with dark brown may give a false impression of the situation. The field of the Williams Medallion carpet (no. 63) has suffered in this way and has been largely reknotted with yarn which has changed colour, and in this class of rugs the same effect may result when yarn is dyed red.

Although many of the colours are still magnificent some fading has occurred.

The range of shades of the various colours and the subtlety with which they are combined are quite remarkable and are outstanding among the rugs of Persia; and yet, recent chemical analyses have proved that the many shades are derived from few substances,[3] which points to exceptionally skilful and meticulous work by dyers utilizing the accumulated lore of their forebears. Comparison of the many shades of colour in various rugs can be made accurately only by means of colour charts, but this is rarely practicable when time is limited. Visual impressions are a poor substitute.

[3] Personal communication from Professor Mark Whiting

Sizes and shapes

[4] Surv. Pl. 1238

So many of the woollen rugs are now reduced that their original sizes cannot be estimated. None are abnormally large when compared with Indo-Persian pieces, some of which are more than sixty feet in length. Even the longest of the dated Sarajevo fragments,[4] which is incomplete, is only just over twenty-eight feet. Small mats, in the European sense, are unknown. Proportions vary from those which are nearly three times as long as they are wide, to others which are relatively broader and much more European in shape, such as the Wagner (no. 1) and Corcoran carpets (no. 15). On the whole many are of good size and there is no doubt that they were produced in an area where large looms were common.

An Oriental shaped or 'fitted' carpet is normally woven in one piece. The loom is dressed in the ordinary way as if for a rectangular carpet but the weaver follows the pattern with whatever unusual angles (no. 38) or curves are required. If the knot counts are equal in both directions there should be no great distortion of the design. When finished, warps, surplus to those needed for fringes, are cut away and, where necessary, raw edges are turned under and felled. Such rugs were used in all walks of life. Thrones, terraces, pavilions and rooms, in octagonal or other shapes, and structures such as tombs or pillars would all require shaped carpets if surfaces and adjoining areas were to be covered satisfactorily. Orders for great carpets of unusual shape would go to well-known weaving centres, but even there the width of what was woven was limited by the width of the loom, and abnormally large carpets, shaped or otherwise, had to be woven in two or more pieces as is still done.

[5] Erdmann 1970 No. 255

[6] Surv. Pl. 1218

The most famous example of a shaped carpet in the 'vase'-technique is the dated piece in the Ethnographical Museum in Sarajevo. Originally it was woven in sections to fit within the tomb chamber as well as around the tomb of Saint Ni'matallāh in the shrine at Mahan some miles to the south-east of Kirman. It is now in seven pieces. Another of somewhat cruciform shape,[5] apparently intended to fill a space between four pillars or other members, is in the Bastan Museum in Tehran. The Spielman fragment[6] in the Victoria and Albert Museum and a lovely fragment (no. 73) from the Denman Ross Collection in the Boston Museum of Fine Arts, which has a tiny remnant of diagonally woven guard stripe, must also have been special orders.

Inscriptions

[7] 1972 text for Pl. 30

Few rugs in the 'vase'-technique are known to have inwoven inscriptions. Again the most famous is the shaped carpet in Sarajevo which has just been mentioned. It bears the name of the master weaver *Ustād Mu'min ibn Qutb al-Dīn Māhānī* and the date 1656 (A.H. 1067) as well as a chronogram. Another signature, overlooked for many years, was recently observed by Dr Ettinghausen[7] in the centre of the famous Sickle-leaf carpet (no. 70) in the Gulbenkian Collection. The signature may be 'Shāhpasand' but because of restoration in this area it is not absolutely certain.

A small fragment with part of an inscription in the Bastan Museum in Tehran may be a third example.

Dating

To appreciate the evolution of ideas concerning dating, and also the provenance, of 'Vase'-technique rugs, opinions of authors, where available, are given in brackets after references to literature and exhibitions. It is interesting to notice how, in the early years of carpet studies, dates in the first half of the sixteenth or even the fifteenth century were assigned to certain carpets. When changes of date were made it was, with rare exceptions, to give one later than that originally suggested, but on the whole the picture is one of repetition of the opinions of the great Islamic scholars of the past, at times with the omission of the question mark which indicated their uncertainty.

Today, interest in Oriental carpets is widespread, and the subject is no longer just the province of Islamic scholars and dedicated connoisseurs. Datable material for the study of textiles is notoriously scanty, and for those who embark on the study of carpets, without grounding in the arts and architecture of Islam, the way is thorny and any evidence for the use of certain motifs or styles at specific times is helpful. Obviously only prolonged study in all branches of Islamic art brings an appreciation of the importance of finer points, but the study of a large group of carpets undoubtedly gives an impression of a sequence of designs, but perhaps no more than an impression. Comparison of the little-known early fragment (no. 50) with the well-known later piece (no. 51) emphasizes the losses of the intervening years and the dangers of theorizing on the evolution of designs.

Good drawing itself is not necessarily indicative of an early period as the graceful design of the Sarajevo carpet of 1656 shows, but good draughtsmanship points to Court patronage. When the finest designs are taken up commercially and reproduced in simplified form and less expensive materials for those of moderate means, constant repetition must result in misunderstood motifs, angular drawing, less subtle colours and coarser weave. Therefore the farther the design is from the prototype the later must be its date and eventually, distorted and misunderstood, it disappears.

Pope[1] pointed out that the long, attenuated figures in one or two of the Sanguszko carpets (nos. 3 and 65) were in the style, rather an original one, of the artist Muḥammadī who flourished shortly after the death of Shāh Tahmasp in 1576. The best of the Sanguszko carpets may, therefore, date from the beginning of the reign of Shāh 'Abbās 1.

[1] Surv. p. 2355

It also seems reasonable to associate the best of the flowering-plant designs with the second quarter of the seventeenth century when the style became widespread in India; and closely related to these are the most graceful of the arabesque designs. Both the vertical alignment and 'squaring off' of the large motifs in three-plane lattice designs and the filling of lattice spaces with multitudinous little flowers give a late impression. This abundance of little flowers occurs in tile designs in the *madrasah* of Ibrāhīm Khān Ẓāhir al-Daulah, governor of Kirman from 1802 to 1824. A large number of Three-plane Lattice rugs survive, which, in itself, indicates a late date, and rather poorly drawn design details reinforce this impression. In addition, the variety of field colours found in somewhat earlier pieces gives way to the monotonous use of red. The idea that 'frozen' borders occur in sixteenth-century carpets is now hardly tenable, and others decorated with broad arabesques in a somewhat ordinary, impoverished style can hardly have been woven before the second half of the seventeenth century. Some may be later. One of the difficulties of dating is deciding which rugs are of the eighteenth century. Trade must have collapsed after the Afghan invasion of 1722. Unfortunately I do not know of any rug in the 'vase'-technique with a traditional design and an inwoven eighteenth-century date, so that there is both reluctance and caution in assigning rugs long regarded as seventeenth century to a much later date. Any distinction between the late seventeenth century and the early eighteenth is difficult to make.

Design

Symbolism

The symbolism of Oriental rug designs has recently been made the subject of a number of articles. Many of the ideas put forward are of great interest, but to attempt to discuss such a subject without a profound knowledge of the philosophies of the East would be unwise, and could easily provide unreliable food for unbridled imaginations. One may believe implicitly in certain things but, especially if they have an ancient religious basis, it may not always be possible to prove them. Such ideas merit attention and to those with a special interest in this aspect of Oriental rugs I recommend the articles by Professor Schuyler van R. Cammann, which are relevant to rugs in the exhibition and are listed in the bibliography.

Classification

Most designs are fairly clear-cut and can be grouped without difficulty for practical purposes of reference, but workshops usually produce more than one type of design and to differentiate between workshops is almost impossible. The exception is the case of certain of the so-called Sanguszko carpets, but not everyone agrees that all the rugs so classified are in fact of the same type. Erdmann[1] was one of these and held the view that if the Berlin Cassirer carpet (no. 64), and what he regarded as a typical Sanguszko, were placed side by side the differences would be convincing. The Buccleuch carpet (no. 7, Plate 4) also raises problems. Among the less well-known rugs examined, three pieces nos. 26/27, the shaped rug in Boston (no. 73) and a handsome fragment in Sarajevo[2] have a flowing style of designs that suggests a specific workshop or another district. There is also a possibility that close comparison will show that certain rugs have unusual technical features in common.

No classification of antique carpets can ever be satisfactory since so much depends on the luck of survival; but the practice of grouping rugs of similar design but different weave, and the habit of referring to the various designs of 'Vase'-technique carpets simply as 'Vase carpets', are so confusing that it makes even a tentative classification desirable.

Inevitably there are pieces which cannot be grouped. One is known which combines sickle leaves clasping palmettes with lobed medallions enclosing animals. Apparently another unusual example has recently been acquired by the Iparmüvészeti Museum in Budapest, and there are others almost certainly of the same weave with unusual designs[3] whose whereabouts are now unknown; but it is felt that most of the usual types have been included in the classification.

[1] 1962a p. 40

[2] Clarke Pl. LXXIX

[3] Surv. Pl. 1232

Designs

'Vase'-technique rugs exhibit one or two unusual features, which are noticeable but not necessarily unique to the type. A surprising number have pictorially arranged elements best viewed from one direction. This perhaps results from the frequent use of figure and animal motifs and naturalistic plants, all of which are inherently pictorial, as well as from the influence of textiles, so many of which have offset directional repeats. Another peculiarity, again perhaps a reflection of a textile style, is the use of false or simulated medallions in which an area such as a lozenge or cartouche is clearly outlined, but the background scrolls continue through it without interruption. Yet a third feature is the frequently encountered narrow main border stripe and the absence of one or even both of the guard stripes.

The most outstanding motifs are animals, large medallions, multiple medallions real or simulated, arabesques, sickle leaves, flowering plants and lattices of leaflets or stems bearing large palmettes, rosettes, vases and similar devices. Large clouds which are such a feature of the designs of some of the great groups of Persian carpets are rare, but the little coiled clouds, either bicoloured and intertwined or monochrome and snail-like, are so frequent that it seems unnecessary constantly to draw attention to them in design descriptions. The popularity of certain specific primary field motifs, and the borders with which they tend to be associated, fluctuates, probably as a reflection of Court taste; but two background patterns, which may or may not incorporate animals, provide a continuity which proceeds to relatively modern rugs. One is a bosky, directional type with or without cypresses, which, for a while, seems to merge with the popular flowering-plant designs. The other is the familiar design known as 'floral scrolls' or 'scrolling vines', which, to some extent, gave way to one of flowering plants.

Borders may be either sections of extensible patterns, as in nos. 14, 24 and 69, or special designs intended to fit a required width as in nos. 2, 3, 30, 51, etc. In animal carpets especially, they are often wide and have guards in proportion and motifs in keeping (nos. 2 and 3), but when, as already mentioned, they are narrow and devoid of guards, they seem quite out of keeping with traditional Persian carpet designing. An explanation which has been suggested is that narrow borders would be appropriate if pairs of carpets were intended to lie side by side.

A number of the designs are based on S-stems variously stylized; and arabesques, either fine and graceful or broad and strap-like, with or without floral scrolls, are among the most popular. Sometimes single flowering plants are arranged directionally one above the other – a common practice in Mughal carpets – or there may be other designs of more intricate or unusual (no. 14) types.

Fine S-stems, progressive vines, reciprocal trefoils, chevron arrangements or even small cartouches are found among the guard stripes, while reciprocal-V or stepped lines provide many sub-guards.

The production of these woollen rugs in such attractive designs seems to have collapsed in the eighteenth century, but many of the motifs and even the designs themselves lived on in other areas (nos. 42 and 58), especially in the Caucasus, in rugs which are structurally distinct; but that is a subject beyond the scope of this catalogue. This may have been due to copying by local weavers or by emigration of weavers from the original centre during difficult times (see p. 70).

Garden carpets

no. 1 (Colour Plate 1)

When the winter capital of the Sasanian Persians (A.D. 224–642) fell to the Arabs in A.D. 637, a remarkable Garden carpet, known as the 'Spring of Chosroes', was found in the great hall of the palace at Ctesiphon, not far from modern Baghdad. It was said to have been of vast size and immense value, but it was cut up and distributed as booty to the troops. The design was that of a garden – always beloved by Persians – but the structure must have been unusual because it is said to have contained jewels. It does, however, provide evidence that such a design was in use at that time, and no doubt it has been woven at intervals ever since. Today this type of formally designed carpet is regarded as a 'bird's eye view' of a garden. The most splendid surviving example,[4] which, from a label, must have been woven before 1632, was found in the palace of the maharajas of Jaipur at Amber.

[4] Dimand 1940

Curiously, the three earliest examples of Garden carpets all differ in their basic plans. The Jaipur carpet has water channels edged with flower beds, a handsome central pavilion, pools, fish, birds and animals, and it has the weave and colouring of so many other pieces in this exhibition. Carpets of this type must have been the prototype for the fairly numerous late provincial Garden carpets, mainly from Northwest Persia. Their designs are highly stylized and largely devoid of animal forms. Martin's somewhat guarded explanation for the presence of such designs in the area was based on information collected in the Middle East in the nineteenth century. He states that in Persia it was averred that in the eighteenth century Nādir Shāh transferred Herat and Kirman weavers to the district around Hamadan. This, if factual, could in part at least explain recognized movements of garden and other designs to Kurdish areas to the north.

[5] Surv. Pl. 1111

The Figdor Garden carpet[5] in Vienna, the best known of the three earliest pieces, is a 'problem' carpet and we regret that it is not in the exhibition for comparison with other rugs. The water channels, animals and medallions all relate it to various designs in 'Vase'-technique rugs, but the unusual arrangements of the motifs and its structure – mainly cotton warps and wefts, and some metal brocading – are not typical of those rugs.

The Wagner carpet (no. 1, Plate 1) differs from both the foregoing in design, but like the Jaipur carpet it is typical structurally.

Centralized designs

nos. 1a, 2 (Colour Plate 2), 3, 4

When a really large medallion, with or without cornerpieces, dominates the centre of a field it is referred to here as a medallion or medallion-and-corner design. Smaller less conspicuous central medallions and cornerpieces, as if part of an offset repeat, are associated with specific types of design but for simplification they are classified with such rugs (nos. 12 and 28) because they give the impression of being introduced simply to provide variety.

Large medallions may be superimposed on extensible field patterns which are limited by the border to the required dimensions. When animals are among the motifs it is more usual to find the design specially planned to fit the area around and between the medallion and the cornerpieces, if the latter are used, with the border overlying little more than a few minor leaflets or stems. This care in designing avoids the undesirable effect of dismembered animals which might result if the medallion and border were simply imposed on an already existing extensible design. The field pattern is, of course, balanced longitudinally and transversely. Sometimes the designs are most pleasing when viewed from the centre of the carpet, at others from the ends.

Medallion rugs in the 'vase'-technique usually have animals in the design (cf. nos. 1a, 2, 3 and 63). The scenes depicted in the Medallion rugs include the famous Paradise parks in which animals, real or mythological, stroll among the trees, engage in combat or flee before the hunt. Cypress trees were popular and they are a feature of some of the most famous of the great Persian Medallion carpets such as the Schwarzenberg[6] and Getty[7] carpets, at present in the Hayward Gallery in London. Both are quite different in weave from the carpets exhibited in Sheffield.

The background designs of one group of Medallion carpets in the 'vase'-technique are purely landscape or scenic (nos. 63 and 1a). A second group has a balanced arrangement of neatly spaced lively animals or combat groups on graceful floral stems (no. 2, Plate 2) used in the same way as large palmettes and other such decorative motifs. This is the group to which most of the Sanguszko carpets belong.

The most impressive of the medallion and landscape designs is the large fragment (no. 63) in the Philadelphia Museum of Art, formerly in the Williams Collection. Apart from comparison of certain design details with those of other carpets, authors seem to have avoided associating it with any specific group of rugs, except for Pope who thought it might be from Tabriz. This apparently was on the basis of the 'cinctured cloudbands' which he regarded as characteristic of that school.

The Williams Medallion carpet is something of a chameleon. About the turn of the century the original dark brown pile of the field, which no doubt had largely worn away, as is the nature of yarn so dyed, was extensively reknotted in green; but, as Martin[7a] remarked, 'a green without life', presumably due to the use of a less lustrous wool for the reknotting. After washing in 1926 the colour changed once more to the present light tobacco brown, in this instance no doubt because of the effect of the washing fluid on a synthetic green dye. The excessive replacement of the pile with the loss of dark brown, which always gives great emphasis to a design, is probably the reason for a certain lack of clarity in the motifs. Certainly more attention has been paid to the border and pendant of this rug than to the field, and no attention at all seems to have been paid to the fact that it has been reknotted and that the weave is similar to so many others in the exhibition. Regrettably the opportunity for comparison is lost as reorganization of the galleries means that this important rug is not available. A Sanguszko carpet, formerly in the Myron C. Taylor

[6] Surv. Pl. 1203
[7] Surv. Pl. 1128

[7a] p. 38

Collection, has, like the foregoing piece, a landscape background devoid of cypresses. The border of the Williams carpet with its reciprocal colour scheme not only relates it to no. 1a but also to the Schwarzenberg carpet, which is differently woven, and to the Chelsea carpet[8] which, being woven on silk, gives little information. But it is perhaps worth a passing thought that the latter carpet, which hangs between two 'Vase'-technique rugs in the Islamic Gallery of the Victoria and Albert Museum, is not so different in colouring from its neighbours.

[8] Surv. Pl. 1130

Multiple-medallion designs

nos. 7 (Colour Plate 4), 66, 67

Offset medallions and compartment repeats, whether the motifs are discrete or linked, overlapping, directional or non-directional, make highly satisfactory carpet designs. When motifs in multiple arrangement predominate they constitute a distinct type, different from those in which medallions are introduced more sparsely and almost as a variant into a design essentially of another type. Pointed medallion-like motifs, plain or lobed, with or without intervening decorative details, and also a great variety of palmettes and other forms, were widespread in textiles of the sixteenth–seventeenth centuries; and in a great silk-producing country at a period when the weaving of luxury silks under royal patronage is well known it is not surprising to find kindred designs in carpets.

The medallions commonly used in 'Vase'-technique carpets are of two types. One is a true superimposed medallion, the other a simulated medallion or enclosure surrounding a primary motif. It is no more than a cartouche, lozenge or other shape in a contrasting colour, but one through which the stems of the design continue without interruption. Like the designs in which medallions with cornerpieces are almost incidental, multiple forms are also at times closely associated with other designs (nos. 52 and 53) and are discussed with them. The type is one which extended far beyond the boundaries of Persia.[9]

[9] Ellis 1962 pp. 33ff.

Pictorially arranged figure or animal scenes in multiple-medallion designs are accompanied by directional subsidiary designs. Of two well-known rugs, the background of one is scenic (no. 7, Plate 4) and that of the other has floral scrolls, palmettes and animals, but the last have the same directional arrangement as the little scenes in the medallions (no. 66). In designs without animals the medallions are simple non-directional offset repeats as in the dated Sarajevo carpet.[10]

[10] Surv. Pl. 1238

The Havemeyer carpet (no. 67) in the Metropolitan Museum, with its transverse and longitudinal rows of superimposed cartouches with colour variation, exemplifies a non-directional type without animals but with simulated medallions. A similar design was also used in Polonaise carpets.[11]

[11] Dimand/Mailey p. 145
[12] Clarke Pl. LXXIX

A long, handsome, blue-ground fragment[12] in Sarajevo, said to have come from a palace in Isfahan, has a series of offset medallions linked with broad, yellow, overlapping arabesques. Although it is of the same construction as the other rugs, the shape of some of the palmettes, the weight of the background stems and the style of drawing are noteworthy.

Directional designs

nos. 10–13 (Colour Plate 5), 14

In directional designs with animals and, sometimes, human figures the arrangement becomes that of little scenes used as individual motifs. The most famous example is the Sanguszko fragment (no. 68) in Paris, now unfortunately too fragile to be moved. In this an elephant and fabulous beasts, as well as scenes from the hunt or incidents from classical Persian literature, all pictorially arranged, make up the design. The suggestion that a central medallion once formed part of this design is unlikely, because, at the longitudinal midline where the border has been rejoined, the head of a dragon, or possibly a *ch'i-lin*, remains. If, in addition to the body of the animal, a medallion had been added, the length of the rug in relation to its width would have been disproportionate.

Other designs, still with bosky backgrounds with cypresses and animals, such as a fragment in East Berlin (no. 69) and nos. 10 and 11, come close to highly complicated textile repeats, but such designs present no problem to the carpet weaver. Repetitive scenic designs persist to later times, particularly in carpets of Northwest Persia and the Caucasus. In these the designs eventually break up and are reduced to scatterings of little animals and angular trees.

Directional designs without animate forms became increasingly popular in the seventeenth century. Those with flowering trees alternating with cypresses – a favourite design in Northwest Persia – are not common in 'Vase'-technique rugs although they are known (no. 14). The popular motif is the flowering plant with which are combined trees reduced to the height of shrubs. In some a willow or a plane may be no taller than an iris (no. 12). The plants vary from naturalistic types to stiffer, 'boteh'-like forms in rigid shapes which speak of constant repetition (no. 13). They may be used alone in offset rows or varied by the addition of medallions and corner-pieces as in no. 12 and also in another well-known rug formerly in the McMullan Collection.[13] When used with arabesque (no. 32) and lattice designs (no. 47) they provide an alternative background to floral scrolls.

[13] Islamic Carpets No. 17

[14] 1941 p. 177

Erdmann[14] suggested that flowering plants followed the floral scrolls and indicated a point in the evolution of the Vase carpets, but he offered neither explanation nor date. Flowering plants of course occur in sixteenth-century Persian carpets, but their arrangement in formal rows, as if in a meticulously laid-out flower bed, is something new. It is the arrangement seen everywhere in the decorative arts of the Shāh Jahān period (1628–58) in India, and the close contact between Persia and India at that time is surely enough to explain the upsurge of such a style in Persia in the second quarter of the seventeenth century.

Sickle-leaf designs

nos. 15 (Colour Plate 6), 16–22

The sickle-leaf motif was popular in rugs from the empire of the Ottomans to the kingdom of the Mughals. In some designs it plays only a minor part, but in others the long, curved, serrated and sometimes compound leaves dominate the field. They may be slim and graceful (no. 15) or sturdy and more angularly curved (nos. 18 and 19) and are borne on swaying stems, at times heavily veined and usually with bracts. One example with medallions and animals is known.

Background designs are either bosky landscapes (nos. 18 and 19) or fine, flowery stems which are often difficult to trace. The sickle leaves, when diagonally opposed, swing around large palmettes or other floral motifs (no. 70). Medallions vary in size and arrangement (nos. 15 and 21) and borders, both broad and narrow, may lack guards.

The group is best known from two magnificent carpets: the Corcoran Throne rug (no. 15, Plate 6), and the Gulbenkian carpet (no. 70) which has a rather unusual type of leaf. The whereabouts of another rug formerly in the Miss Brown Collection[15] in Glasgow is not now known, but a number of fragments, with various border designs, show that this was once a well-known type. So far, attempts to reconstruct larger sections of carpet from some of the fragments have failed, but even small pieces (no. 17) give an idea of the handsome and monumental styles which once prevailed. There is obviously a close relationship between rugs of this group and others with stems organized into superimposed lattices, which bear motifs of a sickle leaf overlying a palmette.[16]

[15] Surv. Pl. 1236

[16] Erdmann 1941 Pl. 18, 24

Arabesque designs

nos. 23–32 (Colour Plates 7 and 8)

Carpets depicted in pre-Safavid as well as Safavid miniatures have designs of broad strap-like arabesques, but only one such rug with a design of animals, and woven in the 'vase'-technique, is widely known. This is the large carpet (no. 71) formerly in the Bardini Collection and now in the Metropolitan Museum of Art. It has recently been referred to as probably from Kurdistan.[17] Two systems of monumental strap-like arabesques extend rhythmically along the wine-red field. Where the tips come together they enclose areas of contrasting colours which simulate medallions. Between the arabesques are animals and fine floral scrolls.

[17] Dimand/Mailey 1973 p. 86

The design of the Metropolitan Museum rug is unusual, but once again fragments such as nos. 23 and 24 provide evidence for the existence at one time of a group of similar pieces.

Broad arabesques without animals are familiar in several silk-pile rugs[18] and in woollen rugs, in particular of the Indo-Persian group,[19] but among 'Vase'-technique rugs I know of them in the field of only one pieced example,[20] now in private possession. It has the quality and colouring of no. 28, Plate 7, and also contains the vases found most often in three-plane lattice designs. Although not usual in field patterns of surviving rugs, broad arabesques appear quite often in borders, especially of lattice designs (nos. 40 and 45).

[18] Surv. Pl. 1252
[19] Erdmann 1961
[20] Hoare p. 10

Other field designs of arabesques vary from graceful arrangements (no. 28, Plate 7) to those with long attenuated forms, usually interlaced and in contrasting colours (no. 32, Plate 8) and yet others in more compact style.[21] There are unusual designs (nos. 26 and 27) including a piece illustrated by Martin[22] which relates to certain of the lattice designs; and there may or may not be superimposed medallions (nos. 28 and 30) or simulated medallions (nos. 26 and 27). Backgrounds are the familiar floral scrolls or flowering plants.

[21] Surv. Pl. 1239
[22] Fig. 185

In this type the most popular border designs consist of arabesque arrangements, but palmettes and floral sprays, graceful or 'frozen', are also found.

Lattice designs

These designs reflect textile styles formed of pairs of undulating stems which come together at regular intervals. In the finest examples the stems curve gracefully and meet to form ogives, but in late rugs they stiffen to rigid diamond shapes. Stem-lattices are either single or of two- or three-plane arrangements superimposed on each other at regular intervals. Normally the design is two ogives wide, and each system bears a variety of decorative motifs.

Three-plane lattice designs

nos. 33, 34 (Colour Plate 9), 39–47 This is the most frequently occurring of the lattice designs. On monochrome fields the stems are not always obvious, particularly if the design is crowded, but they can usually be identified by selecting three of the large motifs aligned vertically, one immediately above the other, and tracing the stems from where they converge and pass under each vertical motif (see no. 47).

The details of the stem-systems, especially in the earlier examples, usually differ. A curved little leaflet which swings first to one side and then to the other is remarkably persistent. Other stems bear conspicuous bracts, a leaflet laid across the stem, or even tiny arabesques or rosettes. The colour and width of the stems, although not always uniform, and the 'veins' all help to distinguish one system from another. Each stem-system bears a variety of decorative motifs such as palmettes, rosettes, irises and sickle leaves overlying palmettes, which, when large, relate the lattice designs to those with sickle leaves and a different stem arrangement. The motifs are executed in varied and attractive colours, but it does not follow that colour symmetry always occurs in balanced motifs.

Sometimes other decorative devices are used, one of which is the vase. More rarely, the designs contain unusual features such as medallions made up of either interlaced arabesques or multicoloured chevron stripes (no. 47), or yet others with smooth contours quite different from the usual palmettes. Even a lozenge formed of four diagonally placed arabesques occurs occasionally. But among these motifs only the vase gave rise to comment, perhaps because western authors recognized and named it more easily than the others. It is also apparent from the literature that the use of the term 'Vase carpet' was a convenient escape from the thorny problem of provenance.

Arrangement of the motifs on the stems varies. All may point in one direction, leaving only large static rosettes to counteract the resulting impression of excessive movement. More often, those on one stem-system point in the opposite direction to those on the others, or the direction of individual motifs on a single stem may vary, but the number of the motifs remains constant. Each lattice bears eight of the large motifs. Four, on conjunctions of stems, lie vertically; the other four diagonally. Each large ogive encloses the six motifs borne by the other two stem-systems. Background decoration in three-plane lattice designs consists of floral scrolls or flowering plants. Borders vary from graceful floral sprays (nos. 34, 37 and 15) to 'frozen' forms. In addition strap-like arabesques, and occasionally also slim graceful ones, are used in various ways, and there are cypresses and flowering plants, four-petal squares and palmettes, and other attractive designs.

These three-plane lattice designs are normally regarded as potentially extensible repeats limited to the required size by the surrounding border; but there is often a pause in the flow of the design. It has been pointed out that the large motifs borne by the stems normally lie either vertically or diagonally according to the position of the stems which bear them, but in rugs with intact field ends palmettes may lie horizontally and are bisected by the border. This seems to occur most often at the beginning of the field. It is not known whether this practice is for the benefit of the designer or the weaver.

Three-plane large-leaf lattice designs

no. 49

In a small group of three-plane lattice designs one of the stem-systems becomes unusually prominent due to the placing of long, serrated or compound leaves on the diagonal stretches of the stems, instead of the customary more compact floral motifs which are still borne by the other two stem-systems. The use of contrasting colours in adjoining spaces makes the lattice of large leaves even more prominent. In a fragment of such a rug in the Musée des Arts Décoratifs in Paris[23] the leaves are graceful and follow the slightly curved stems which they overlie, but in most examples they are rather straight and form lozenges rather than ogives. The spaces contain either the usual six, or sometimes only four, motifs – two vertical and two horizontal (no. 49). In the latter the stems turn somewhat abruptly instead of following a gentle curve. Occasionally a space is entirely filled with parallel lines of multicoloured chevron stripes. Backgrounds are decorated with floral scrolls.

[23] Inv. 27656

Borders of S-stems terminating in floral sprays can be followed through graceful and slightly stylized[24] forms to the frequently occurring 'frozen' forms. Broad arabesques are also used.

[24] Clarke Pl. XCIII

Originally it was suggested that the famous Dragon carpets of the Caucasus, with their great lattices of overlapping, serrated leaves, were the prototypes for the Vase carpets, but the logical movement of designs is from a great weaving centre to a more provincial one. Furthermore, the evidence is that Caucasian designers not only lack originality but also have a great facility for purloining designs, especially those of 'Vase'-technique rugs, which means that the Caucasian rugs are the copies rather than the prototypes.

Some sort of large-leaf lattice design such as occurs in rugs of this group, but with the addition of animal motifs – and enough has been said to show that animals are by no means rare in 'Vase'-technique carpets – may well have been the prototype for the Dragon carpet designs.

Two-plane leaflet-lattice designs

nos. 50–53

Another small group of rugs has two-plane leaflet-lattice designs which can be further subdivided into two main groups. Some, like the large-leaf lattice designs, have contrasting colours in adjoining spaces, others have monochrome fields.

In the first type the primary lattice which encloses the different colours is formed, so far as is known, only by the small leaflet stems. In the centre of each space is a single large motif which covers the conjunctions of the secondary stem-system. Compared with the spaces of three-plane lattice designs, these are small. An early example (no. 50) shows the gracefulness of such a design.

The rugs of the second type have monochrome fields and rather plain lattice stems with or without a few bracts or other small devices. They give the impression of a multi-medallion design but, as the motifs are simulated instead of true medallions, the design is basically that of a two-plane lattice. The designer has created variety by enclosing the usual vertical motifs of one (no. 52) or both (no. 53) stem-systems in lozenges or other outlines, but this forms no barrier to the stems which converge, pass beneath the central motif and re-emerge to continue their usual course along the field.

Single-plane lattice designs

nos. 54–58

Such designs may be extremely attractive, but, as with the previous group, the rugs have not survived in such large numbers as those in three-plane lattice patterns.

The lattices are formed in various ways. They may be composed of single stems with bracts enlarged to calyx-like forms (no. 55, Plate 11), arabesques (nos. 54 and 72) or leaves (no. 57).

These designs are directionally arranged and contain flowering plants in the spaces, with the exception of no. 58. Borders are broad, decorated with arabesques and have both outer and inner guard stripes.

One of the finest designs (no. 72), surrounded by a richly decorated border, deserves special mention. It consists of a lattice of graceful arabesques, each space of which encloses beautifully drawn flowering plants or an occasional vase and bracket. The whereabouts of the fragment illustrated, once owned by Professor Sarre, are unknown, but from the photograph it looks much better preserved than a large fragment in Boston,[25] another in the Burrell Collection[26] put together from small fragments, and a third piece in Paris[27] in which the arabesques have been worked over in red yarn.

[25] Bode/Kühnel Pl. 58 No. 100
[26] Inv. 9–22
[27] Erdmann 1960 No. 75

Provenance and dating given for one or other of the fragments are Northern or Central Persia sixteenth century; seventeenth century; Joshagan; Kirman (?) sixteenth century; perhaps sixteenth century; but because of the naturalism of the flowering plants and the elegance of the design as a whole, a date in the second quarter of the seventeenth century seems most likely.

Even in the twentieth century Bakhtiari women still weave large carpets in this design, but peacocks, cypresses, full-blown roses and other floral forms replace the plants of the earlier rugs. A forgery of small size is known.

Glossary

Technical

Z or S
The direction of the twist of the fibres of a single strand of spun yarn, when viewed vertically, conforms either to the diagonal of the letter Z or to that of the letter S. The same symbols are used for the direction of two or more strands of yarn when twisted together (plied). In hand-spun yarn the ply is usually opposite in direction to that of the spin.

2Z or 2S
Two strands of Z-spun yarn or of S-spun yarn lying together but not plied.

Z2S
Z-spun yarn, two strands of which are S-plied, and by analogy Z5S, S4Z, etc.

U
Yarn, apparently unspun, or in which the direction is undetermined. This is not unusual in silk.

w
Winder-plied as in Z2Sw, i.e. Z-spun yarn, two strands of which are only loosely S-plied. This loose ply is effected by winding strands of yarn into a ball from rotatable winders. Such yarn is commonly used in the pile and in the wefts of many rugs. As the twist of the plied yarn may occur only at wide intervals, yarn which appears to be 2Z may in fact be winder-plied.

foundation
The basis or groundwork of a carpet formed of a plain weave of warps to which knots are attached, and wefts which hold them in position. It determines the strength of a carpet.

warp
Yarns, tightly spun and plied for strength, which extend from end to end of the rug and around which the knots are tied. The cut ends usually form the fringes at the ends of a rug. Warps may lie in one plane or in two. If the lower layer is visible between the warps of the upper layer the weave is said to be 'depressed' (D).

weft
Yarns, which are passed from side to side of a rug above each row of knots. They are usually loosely spun and unplied or only lightly plied, in order to pack down well on the knots and hold them in position.

× 3 etc.
The number of passes of weft after each row of knots.

knots
As used in carpet literature the term 'knot' denotes the interlacement around the warps of yarn which forms the pile of the rug. Because the ends are not twisted about each other and drawn tight as in a true knot the term is a misnomer. The *asymmetrical* (Persian, Senna) knot (fig. A) open on the left is the one commonly found in great

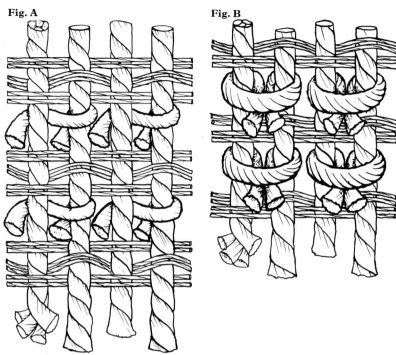

Fig. A **Fig. B**

Persian carpets of the classical period. When tied over four warps, instead of two, it is known as the *jufti* (paired) or false knot, the latter name derived from the fact that, in total, the rug requires less yarn, and in consequence the pile lacks density and wears poorly. The *symmetrical* (Turkish, Gördes) knot (fig. B) is rarely tied on more than two warps.

knot count	The number of knots per linear inch (2.5 cm) transversely, multiplied by the number per linear inch longitudinally, gives the count per square inch. Where the metric system is in use the linear count is based on the decimetre (10 cm or 4 in).
pile	The soft velvety surface of a carpet formed by the projecting knot yarn. It is usually cut but may be looped.
shag	A long, loose pile attached, in carpets, to the back plane of warps, for the purpose of providing additional warmth and softness.
brocading	Supplementary wefts introduced to produce a special effect or pattern. They are used in specific areas and do not extend from one side of the rug to the other.
flat-weave	A kilim or similar fabric without pile.
layout of carpet design	See fig. C.
Vase carpet	A confusing term, loosely used to refer to carpets in a variety of designs, some of which contain vase motifs. Not all pieces to which this term is applied are constructed in the same way.
'vase'-technique	The method of construction of many of the so-called Vase carpets. For details see p. 14 and foldout inside back cover.
'Vase'-technique carpets	The name given to any carpet woven in the above technique, irrespective of design.

General

arabesque

Decoration, characteristic of Islamic art, used here to indicate split-leaf forms one of which often grows from the tip of another.

boteh

A leaf-like motif with curved tip, most familiar in the West as the 'pear' motif of Paisley shawls.

cartouche

A decorative panel.

ch'i-lin or kylin

A mythological creature of various forms, used here to indicate a deer-like animal with a bushy tail; derived from Chinese decorative art.

clouds

Motifs of various forms – asymmetrical, symmetrical, or coiled. The latter, in rug literature, are often referred to as 'chi' or 'tschi'.

'frozen' border

Sprays of tiny flowers or buds so stylized that they form stiff little rows arranged as rectangles. They usually terminate S-stems (q.v.) and are used in borders or guards.

Fig. C

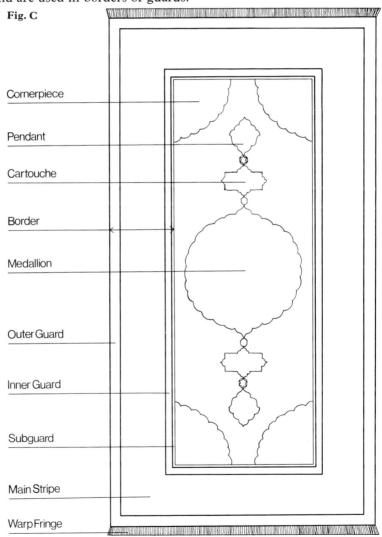

Cornerpiece

Pendant

Cartouche

Border

Medallion

Outer Guard

Inner Guard

Subguard

Main Stripe

Warp Fringe

kilim (Pers. *gelim*)	A rug without pile, tapestry-woven and weft-faced.
'Kufic' border	Meaningless interlaced design (used for centuries in carpet borders) derived from an early form of angular Arabic writing known as Kufic script. The name is taken from the town of Kufa in Iraq.
lozenge	A motif with equal sides, having two acute and two obtuse angles. It may be lobed or stepped.
ogive	A rounded motif with pointed ends formed of convex and concave lines.
palmette	A fan-like motif probably named from the resemblance to the spreading fronds of a palm tree.
Sanguszko carpets	Carpets of similar style named after a handsome Medallion-and-corner carpet in the possession of Prince Sanguszko, which is at present exhibited in the Metropolitan Museum, New York. It was first shown in Leningrad in 1904 and is said to have been taken at the battle of Chocim in 1621.
	The following are illustrated in the catalogue: no. 2, Plate 2, the Béhague; no. 3, Textile Museum, Washington; no. 7, Plate 4, Buccleuch; no. 64, the Cassirer; no. 65, Victoria and Albert Museum; no. 66, Lyons; no. 69, East Berlin.
	For illustrations of others see: *Survey*, Plates 1205 (Taylor); 1206 (Sanguszko), 1207, no. 1b (Madrid), and Benguiat, no. 53; Sarre & Martin IV, no. 23 (Kelekian; Mumford Plate XVIII (Yerkes/Trevor).
sickle leaf	A long curved leaf with serrated edge.
S-stems	One of the commonest decorative devices in borders and guards consists of contiguous stems of S-shape. Small floral motifs terminate the stems and larger forms such as palmettes or rosettes are placed on the diagonals and on the points of contact of adjoining S-stems. The order given in descriptions is terminals, diagonals and contacts.
Surv.	Abbreviation for *A Survey of Persian Art* by Arthur Upham Pope and Phyllis Ackermann, 1939.

Plate 1 (cat. no. 1). The Wagner Garden Carpet, Burrel Collection, Glasgow.

Plate 2 (cat. no. 2). The Béhague Sanguszko Medallion Carpet. Thyssen-Bornemisza Collection, Lugano.

Plate 3 (cat. no. 5). The Peytel Small Silk Kashan Carpet.
Musée du Louvre, Paris.

te 4. (cat. no. 7). Multiple-medallion Carpet. Duke of
cleuch and Queensberry, VRD.

Plate 5 (cat. no. 13). Flowering-plant design, directionally arranged. Textile Museum, Washington, DC.

Plate 6 (cat. no. 15). The Corcoran Throne Rug in a sickle-leaf design. Corcoran Gallery of Art, Washington, DC.

Plate 7 (cat. no. 28). Arabesque design with medallion and cornerpieces. Burrell Collection, Glasgow.

Plate 8 (cat. no. 32). Arabesque design with flowering plants. Firma Bernheimer, Munich.

Plate 9 (cat. no. 34). Three-plane lattice design with a background of scrolling stems, a so-called Vase carpet. Museum für Islamische Kunst, Berlin-Dahlem.

Plate 10 (cat. no. 49). Three-plane large-leaf lattice design with different colours in the spaces, a so-called Vase carpet. Textile Museum, Washington, DC.

Plate 11 (cat. no. 55). Single-plane lattice design with flowering plants directionally arranged. Kunstmuseum, Düsseldorf.

Plate 12 (not exhibited). Polonaise carpet showing the brilliant colours that must have characterized many such rugs in the seventeenth century. Compare with other silk carpets in the exhibition: nos. 5 (Plate 3), 6 and 8.

Catalogue

Catalogue notes

In measurements, width is given before length, which is the sequence in weaving, and outer guards are described before inner. For technical details of individual rugs, see foldout.

For the use of terms Vase carpet, 'vase'-technique, etc., see Glossary, p. 30.

Provenance and dates given in brackets under Literature and Exhibitions are explained on p. 17.

The carpets are not necessarily hung as illustrated, but as far as possible they are arranged so that the beginning of the weave is at the lower end.

Two collections recently dispersed contained numerous carpets and fragments relevant to rugs in this exhibition. The Baranovicz Collection is said to have been sold privately comparatively recently after the death of the owner some years ago. It is known to me only from photographs. Much of the Erlenmeyer Collection was sold at Sotheby's in 1972.

1

1 (Colour Plate 1)

The Wagner Garden Carpet; a design of trees, water channels, fish, animals, birds and butterflies on a deep blue field. Yellow border with overlapping S-stems ending in small sickle leaves; red and blue reciprocal, and red, guards.

Woollen-pile carpet, late 17th century.
Width: 432 cm (14 ft 2 in)
Length: 531 cm (17 ft 5 in)

The Burrell Collection, Glasgow Art Gallery and Museum, Inv. 9–2.

This famous carpet came to light in Istanbul at the turn of the century and Martin regarded it as 'a vivid illustration of the Spring Carpet of Chosroes'.[1] It represents an enclosed plantation rather than a conventional garden with flower beds, and the network of water lines also differs from the usual parallel and diverging arrangement used to indicate moving water. Many of the trees have the thick boles which appear in classical Court carpets and in stylized designs of later pieces differently woven. Only two Garden carpets in typical 'vase'-technique are known, but Martin[2] illustrated a fragment with such a tree which may be from another one.

The crowding of the design with little flowers, the rather poorly drawn animals much reduced in size, the inconspicuous vases on flattened brackets, all point to a rather late date.

The absence of transverse symmetry and the somewhat square shape may mean that only part of a cartoon, intended for a much longer carpet, was used here.

Pope considered that the small coiled 'clouds' and vine-leaf palmette in the border related this carpet to the Sanguszko group, but in 1941 Erdmann was not convinced of this. Latterly he regarded it as North Persian. In 1961 the observation that it was structurally the same as various Vase carpets pointed once more to Martin's original suggestion that it might be Kirman work.

[1] p. 81
[2] Fig. 201

Coll: R. Wagner, Berlin
      USA
      J.A. Holms, Glasgow
Lit: 1908 Martin p. 81 Fig. 200 (Kirman c.1640)
     1913 Conway p. 96 (quotes Martin)
     1921 Sarre p. 113
     1922 Kendrick & Tattersall, pp. 12 103 Pl. 3 (16th–17th century)
     1929 Kendrick p. 26 Fig. 5
     1939 Surv. pp. 2355 2451 (inclines to group it with the Sanguszko carpets)
     1940 Dimand p. 93
     1941 Erdmann p. 170
     1958 Bode/Kühnel p. 142 Ill. 104
     1959 Dilley Pl. v (Persia c.1600)
     1961 Beattie p. 6 (technically related to Vase carpets)
     1962b Erdmann p. 40 Ill. 9 (North Persia beginning 18th century)
     1964 Spuhler p. 593 (close connection with Vase carpets late 17th century)
     1968 Beattie p. 5
     1970 Erdmann p. 70 Fig. 74 (North Persia beginning 18th century)
Exh: 1949 Glasgow (827)
     1951 Glasgow (34)
     1964 Leeds (22) (Beattie: technically related to rugs of Kirman 17th century)
     1969 Glasgow (9) (South Persian 17th century)
     1975 London (286) (possibly Kirman 17th century)

1a (this exhibit unfortunately not now available)

The Stieglitz Carpet. A centralized design with a large red medallion on a blue field, decorated with a Paradise scene of flowering trees, cypresses, fabulous creatures and clouds. Reciprocal red and ivory border main stripe between yellow and orange guards.

Woollen-pile carpet fragment, late 16th century.
Width: 262 cm (8 ft 6 in)
Length: 251 cm (6 ft 4 in)

The Hermitage Museum, Leningrad, Inv. 7504.

Apparently this carpet has not previously been exhibited in Western Europe. According to Sarre and Trenkwald it was illustrated as Plate XVIII in a little-known catalogue of the Hermitage Museum in 1925. Pope grouped it with Tabriz carpets although the plate in the *Survey* bears the caption 'Kirman (?)'.

The Stieglitz carpet appears to have the weave and the colouring of many 'Vase'-technique carpets, and there seems no reason why a handsome design of this type should not be produced in several centres. Indeed such medallion designs with scenic backgrounds occur in the Mantes[1] and the Getty Crane carpet[2] which technically could be from Northwest Persia, in the Schwarzenberg carpet[3] which differs in structure and 'handle' and in the Paris/Cracow fragments which Pope regarded as Tabriz work but which are entirely on silk and more recently have been assigned to East Persia[4].

[1] Surv. Pl. 1127
[2] Surv. Pl. 1128
[3] Surv. Pl. 1203
[4] Ellis 1965 pp. 47 54 Pl. 7a

Coll: Stieglitz
Lit: 1926 Sarre and Trenkwald II Pl. 21
     1939 Surv. p. 2308 2385 Pl. 1204A (groups with Tabriz rugs, end 16th century)
     1941 Erdmann p. 158
     1957 Kühnel p. 8 Ill. 4
     1962a Erdmann p. 40

1b (not illustrated)

A medallion-and-corner design in which a lobed, eight-pointed, yellow medallion containing paired fish biting duck, and dark blue cornerpieces each with a dragon and phoenix combat, constitute the primary motifs, on a red field. Lively animals, single or in combat, and graceful floral scrolls, decorate the field between the large motifs. Broad red S-stems on the ivory main stripe of the border terminate in short, heavy arabesques and bear yellow palmettes with a single animal on the diagonals, and lobed blue ogives with combat scenes on the points of contact, of the stems. Eroded brown outer, and yellow inner, guards.

Woollen-pile carpet, late 16th century.
Width: 215 cm (7 ft)
Length: 430 cm (14 ft 1 in)

Instituto Valencia de Don Juan, Madrid.

In 1932 Erdmann grouped this carpet with those other pieces, similar in style, which came to be known as the Sanguszko carpets (cf p. 32). It has the colouring, the gracefully drawn animals and foliage, the richly ornamented style and the handsome border which characterize such carpets. In 1941 he suggested an origin in Kashan (cf p. 12) rather than in Yazd or in Kirman which were the alternatives favoured by Pope. Later Kühnel, in an article drawing attention to the occurrence in a number of rugs of motifs such as paired fish and paired birds, pointed out that the designs probably originated in a court manufactory in Northwest Persia in the first half of the sixteenth century, and that at a later date the combining of motifs in different ways resulted in the luxuriant style characteristic of the Sanguszko group. He tentatively assigned these rugs to Qazvin, the capital of the Safavid empire in the second half of the sixteenth century.

Superficially the Madrid carpet is more typical of the Sanguszko group than either the Buccleuch (no. 7, Plate 4) or the Cassirer (no. 64) carpets. To judge from notes all three seem to differ slightly in weave from the usual 'Vase'-technique rugs.

Lit: 1932 Erdmann pp. 710 722 Ill. p. 711 (beginning 17th century)
  1939 Surv. p. 2351 Pl. 1207 (Kirman or Yazd)
  1941 Erdmann p. 170 (suggests Kashan)
  1957 Kühnel p. 8 Ill. 6 (detail) (Qazvin ?, towards end of 16th century)
  1960 Erdmann p. 44 Ill. 88 (Central Persia (Kashan) c.1600)
Exh: 1931 London (249 according to catalogue description; not 113 as stated in Surv. Pl. 1207 and elsewhere)

2

2 (Colour Plate 2)

The Béhague Sanguszko Carpet. Medallion and animal design with floral scrolls on an ivory field; conspicuous motifs on the midline extend towards the end of the rug from the lobed red medallion. Red border, with animal medallions alternating with phoenix and *ch'i-lin* combats, between ivory and pale yellow guards.

Woollen-pile carpet, Shāh ʿAbbās period.
Width: 275 cm (9 ft)
Length: 509 cm (16 ft 8½ in)

Thyssen-Bornemisza Collection, Lugano, Switzerland, Inv. 669a.

As far as is known this carpet has never previously been exhibited, and until recently has been known only from a monochrome photograph, which may explain why it has been little discussed.

The design, best viewed from the ends, is devoid of cornerpieces, and as one would expect in a carpet with a large central medallion, the field pattern is symmetrical in both directions, but unlike the Williams (no. 63) and Hermitage (no. 1a) medallion fragments and the Taylor carpet, all with scenic designs, the background in this case is composed of floral scrolls with animals which are used in the same way as floral motifs. This is the most common form of background pattern in the Sanguszko group as the designs of no. 3, the Benguiat, Madrid (no. 1b), Sanguszko, Yerkes/Trevor and Victoria and Albert (no. 65) carpets show; it is also used in the Cassirer carpet (no. 64) which is usually associated with this group.

Coll: Countess de Béhague (formerly de Béarn), Paris
Marquis de Ganay, Paris
Rosenberg & Stiebel
Lit: 1939 Surv. pp. 2349 2353 2451 (Kirman or Yazd; Pl. 1210; Kirman late 16th century)
1941 Erdmann p. 169f. (Kashan?)
1957 Kühnel p. 11 (problem of origin of Sanguszko group still open; Qazvin possibly, towards end of 16th century)
1958 Bode/Kühnel p. 107 (Qazvin? towards end of 16th century)
1958 Heinemann p. 149 (Persian early 17th century)
1972 Beattie p. 27 (may be early 17th century)

3

Medallion-and-corner design with animals, with a background of floral scrolls bearing palmettes containing masks, on a pale yellow field. Animal combat groups lie between handsome blue serrated leaves which swing out from large floral motifs on the red border. Yellow guards with animal, and with floral, decoration.

Woollen-pile carpet fragment, Shāh ʿAbbās period.
Width: 120 cm (3 ft 11½ in)
Length: 77 cm (2 ft 6 in)

Textile Museum, Washington, D.C., Inv. R 33.2.1.

This is part of a Medallion-and-corner carpet of the Sanguszko group, but only the tip of a cornerpiece remains. Two more pieces are in the Textile Museum. One[1] is almost a mirror image of this but without border; the other[2] is the right upper corner of the border. These, another corner fragment formerly in the Kelekian Collection,[3] and a tiny piece of border in the Boston Museum of Fine Arts may all be from the same carpet. Like the medallion here, the cornerpiece of the Kelekian fragment also contains tall, slim, winged figures, a motif which occurs in the Sanguszko carpet itself and in the large fragment (no. 65) in the Victoria and Albert Museum which is probably the earliest of the group. A number of other features link these carpets, such as the large leaves in the border, paired fish and peacocks and certain guard stripes.

[1] Inv. 69.11.3
[2] Inv. 69.11.2
[3] Sarre and Martin IV No. 23

Coll: Kelekian
Lit: 1912 Sarre and Martin supp. vol. IV. 23
1957 Kühnel Ill. 7 (compares with Cassirer carpet. Problem of origin of group still open; possibly Qazvin towards end of 16th century)
1968 Ellis Fig. 14 (Kirman or Kirman weavers working elsewhere)
Exh: 1910 Munich (23) (Sarre: Persian 16th century)

3

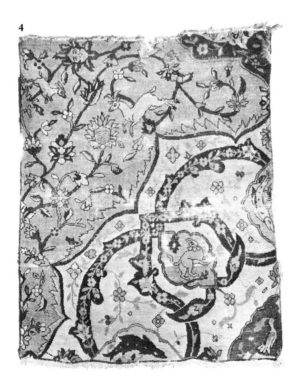

4

5

4

Weaver's pattern (?). Medallion and animal design in the manner of a Sanguszko carpet, on a red field.

Woollen-pile carpet, 19th century.
Width: 127 cm (4 ft 2 in)
Length: 160 cm (5 ft 3 in)

John Hewett.

This rug has never been any wider and is complete at the medallion end. Compared with the Sanguszko carpets it has all-cotton warps and wefts and a restricted colour range.

In design it is closest to the Victoria and Albert Museum's Sanguszko fragment (no. 65) which was acquired in 1883, but the medallion arabesques are narrower and there is an undue amount of space between them. The animal in the lobed lozenge is reversed, and the combat scene adjoining the medallion is missing. Palmettes on the floral stems contain masks but the stems do not scroll as in a Sanguszko carpet (cf. no. 3).

Many classical carpet designs were copied from the late nineteenth century onwards, usually for household use with no intent to deceive, but sometimes as forgeries; but it is unusual to find what may have been a weaver's sample. It can hardly have been the intention to grind this down and pass it off as an antique fragment because it is obviously wrong in both design and colour. It is equally difficult to see how the field, as designed, could have been satisfactorily extended as in a Sanguszko carpet proper, or to believe that an Oriental designer would fail properly to reproduce scrolling vines. This leaves the possibility that the design may have been supplied by one of the European commercial establishments in Persia.

Coll: Private, Tangier, 1950–72

5 (Colour Plate 3)

The Peytel Small Silk Carpet of Kashan in a design of animals and flowering plants on a blue field. Animal masks in lotus palmettes alternate with unusual floral motifs on a red border. S-stems with bicoloured leaves, a palmette and rosette decorate the ivory outer guard, and a similar more simplified design is used on the inner guard, also ivory.

Silk-pile carpet, 16th century.
Width: 124 cm (4 ft)
Length: 109 cm (3 ft 7 in)

Musée du Louvre, Paris (Peytel gift 1914), Inv. 6741.

A group of these small silk-pile carpets of beautiful quality and design has for years been assigned to Kashan.[1] This famous carpet is exhibited, not only for its beauty, but also for comparison of colours and drawing with those of the woollen carpets with animal designs which Erdmann believed came from Kashan (see p. 12).

The skill of craftsmen seems to have varied and those who dyed the yarns for the Silk Carpets of Kashan were more adept at fixing pigments on silk than those who dyed the yarns for the weavers of the Polonaise carpets, some of which are assigned to Kashan and others to Isfahan. The colours of the former group – both Large and Small – are still often intense, but fading does occur to some extent as examination of the often described salmon-coloured field of the Vienna Hunting carpet shows. It was once brilliant red. Comparison with what are believed to be the original brilliant colours of a Polonaise presents difficulties as so many have faded, but Plate 12 gives an idea of what these colours must once have been like.

[1] Surv. p. 2344

Coll: Hakky Bey
      Joanny Peytel
Lit: 1894 Marye (Persian 15th century)
      1903a Migeon p. 18 (Persian 16th century)
      1903b Migeon Pl. 75 (Persian 16th century)
      1903 Sarre p. 336 (16th century)
      1922 Migeon No. 124 Pl. 35 (16th century)
      1927 Migeon II p. 375 Fig. 451 (Persian 16th century)
      1929 Sarre & Trenkwald Pl. 40 (Persian second half 16th century)
      1957 Pinder-Wilson No. 80 (Kashan? 16th century)
      1970 Erdmann p. 188 No. 233 (Kashan 16th century)
Exh: 1893 Paris
      1903 Paris (663) (Persian 15th century)
      1938 Paris, Bibliothèque Nationale (191)
      1971 Paris (4) (Kashan 16th century)

5a

5a

Polonaise carpet with a small segment of an extensible design composed of transverse rows of cartouches alternating with rows of octafoils and arabesque medallions. The former are linked by curved stems, the latter occupy the centre of the field and the corners. Alternately reversed pairs of arabesques rise from palmettes in the main border between narrow floral guard stripes.

Silk-pile carpet with metal brocading, 17th century.
Width: 122 cm (4 ft)
Length: 208 cm (6 ft 10 in)

His Grace The Duke of Buccleuch and Queensberry, VRD, Inv. No. 9.

This rug, with remains of extensive brocading done with silk yarn wrapped with gold or silver strip, exemplifies the rich materials used in the production of these carpets for which Persia was so famous in the seventeenth century. Although the original colours of this and the carpet illustrated in Plate 12 were not necessarily the same, a comparison of the two gives an idea of changes which have occurred in the course of time in many of these pieces.

Coll: Dukes of Buccleuch
Lit: 1950   Hamburg (Erdmann) (89)
      1957   Erdmann p. 579
      1968a Spuhler No. 124 (Isfahan first quarter 17th century)
Exh: 1914   London (40) Pl. IX (Persian c. 1600)
      1931   London (346)
      1964   Leeds (29) (Persian 17th century)

6

The Doistau Kilim. The yellowish lobed medallion and cornerpieces with scenes of figures and animals dominate a mid-blue field decorated with animals and flowers. In the main border stripe the broad stems of heavy outpointing red, and inpointing blue-green, arabesques overlie ivory palmettes which still show traces of metal-covered yarn. The ivory guards contain cartouches of various colours linked by quatrefoils.
Silk tapestry-woven kilim enriched with metal-covered silk, 17th century.
Width: 139 cm (4 ft 5½ in)
Length: 249 cm (8 ft 1½ in)

Musée du Louvre, Paris (Doistau gift 1904), Inv. No. 5946.

It is known from documents that the King of Poland, Sigismund III Wasa ordered carpets in, and received them from, Kashan at the beginning of the seventeenth century, and several silk tapestry-woven carpets containing the Polish arms, always presumed to be part of that order, have been preserved. From those and other documents referring to the weaving of silk in Kashan it is usually assumed that surviving kilims were woven in that city, although apart from the armorial kilims there is no evidence for assuming that they all came from one centre.

Unlike the silk-pile Polonaise carpets a number of the kilims have animals and figures in the designs.

Pope interpreted the medallion scene as Bahrām Gūr and the Dragon, an incident from Firdawsi's *Shāh Nāmah* or Book of Kings, in which are described the exploits of the great national heroes of Persia; and those in the cornerpieces as the lovers Laylah and Majnūn. Erdmann regarded this as a Kashan kilim and to support his belief in a Kashan origin for the Sanguszko carpets he compared the border with those of the Taylor, Madrid (no. 1b) and Lyons (no. 66) carpets, and the corner scenes with those in the Paris Sanguszko carpet (no. 68).

Coll: M. Doistau
Lit: 1903a Migeon p. 24 (Persian 16th century)
      1903b Migeon Pl. 72 (Persian 16th century)
      1911   D'Allemagne opp. p. 94
      1922   Kendrick & Tattersall, p. 33 Pl. 26 (Persian 17th century)
      1922   Migeon 126 Pl. 37
      1927   Migeon p. 372, Fig. 452 (Persian 16th century)
      1932b Erdmann p. 228
      1935   Dimand p. 21 No. 10 (most likely provenance Isfahan first half 17th century)
      1939   Surv. p. 2405, Pl. 1262 (Kashan end 17th century)
      1941   Erdmann p. 169f. (Kashan)
      1968a Spuhler p. 241 W.14 (Kashan first quarter 17th century)
      1971   Ettinghausen p. 74 No. 31 (Persian c. 1600)
Exh: 1903   Paris (677)
      1935   New York Metropolitan Museum (10)
      1937   Chicago (236)
      1938   Paris, Bibliothèque Nationale (188)

7 (Colour Plate 4)

Multiple-medallion carpet with offset rows of pointed lobed medallions and cartouches linked longitudinally by roundels. Figural scenes in most medallions, birds or palmettes in the cartouches and animals and trees in the intervening spaces, are arranged on a red field. Cartouches containing dragon-and-phoenix combats are linked to intertwined dragons on a dark blue border; red and ivory guards with animal decoration.

Woollen-pile carpet, 17th century.
Width: 226 cm (7 ft 5 in)
Length: 452 cm (14 ft 10 in)

His Grace The Duke of Buccleuch and Queensberry, VRD, Inv. 12.

In 1932, after the London exhibition of Persian art, Erdmann drew attention to similar characteristics in a number of carpets which came to be known as the Sanguszko group. The arguments he used in favour of a Kashan origin are listed on p. 12. Among the points he made was the similarity of the design plan of this carpet to that of the Figdor silk kilim (no. 8), one of the group regarded as coming from Kashan.

A striking feature of the Buccleuch carpet is the dragon-and-phoenix combat in the border cartouches. This is the form of dragon which, in more angular drawing, was used in the Dragon carpets of the Caucasus.

In his review of the Leeds Exhibition, Spuhler considered that one of the problems raised by the exhibition was the possibility of a later dating for this carpet.

Little attention has been paid to Kendrick's original information[1] on the history of the Boughton treasures. Ralph, Duke of Montagu, ancestor of the present owner, and Ambassador Extraordinary to Louis XIV, entered Paris in 1669 'in a manner so magnificent that it has scarce ever since been equalled'. In 1690 he returned from France and, inspired by Versailles, altered, and added to, Boughton, and furnished it with a rich collection of works of art. In 1684 King William III had created him Earl of Montagu. That was the very year in which Engelbert Kaempfer was in Isfahan and reported the use, at Court, of Kirman woollen carpets in animal designs.

In Northwest Persia such designs, some with early features, were apparently still current. A Persian embroidery, regarded as seventeenth-eighteenth century on the basis of a later datable piece, has features similar to those of this carpet.[2] The figures even wear the stick turban fashionable in the sixteenth century. The compartments of the embroidery have the same band-outlines as those in some Northwest Persian carpets and they also appear here and in the Sanguszko rug formerly in the Yerkes/Trevor Collections. The somewhat hard drawing of the carpet design, to

which Bode/Kühnel[3] called attention not long after it became known, might therefore be explained not only by production in another centre but also by a rather later date than that with which it is usually credited.

Shortly before the completion of this catalogue the opportunity came to re-examine the Buccleuch carpet. In the light of experience gained since it was exhibited in Leeds in 1964 it seems thinner and more pliable, in spite of the good condition of the pile, than many of the 'Vase'-technique rugs. The most striking feature, however, is the conspicuous orange second weft. The possibility should be considered that this may be a seventeenth-century copy in the manner of a Sanguszko rug but woven in a different area.

7

It should be noted that Pope's analysis of this carpet, in which he reports an all-silk foundation, is not correct. The silk warps used to give a richer finish to the ends run into the body of the rug only for some five or six inches. The rest of the warps are cotton. The practice of adding a silk fringe is not unusual in Polonaise and Indo-Persian rugs, but it is unusual among 'Vase'-technique rugs.

The views on provenance and dating expressed by various authors are indicative of the problems presented by this carpet.

[1] London 1914 p. 17
[2] Wace Ill. 4
[3] 1922 p. 16

Coll: Dukes of Buccleuch
Lit: 1914 Kendrick No. 29 Pl. 7 (Persian 17th century)
      1922 Kendrick & Tattersall p. 27 Pl. 22 (Persian 16th–17th century)
      1922 Bode/Kühnel p. 16 Ill. 19
      1929 Sarre & Trenkwald II, text to Pl. XVII
      1930 Kühnel p. 464
      1931 Erdmann p. 661 & note 20
      1931 Tattersall p. 9
      1932a Erdmann p. 722 Ill. p. 716
      1939 Surv. p. 2357 Pl. 1209 (Yazd or Kirman) p. 2451 (Kirman late 16th century)
      1941 Erdmann p. 170 (Kashan)
      1955 Bode/Kühnel p. 130 Ill. 94 (related to Kirman or Kashan medallion group, i.e. Sanguszko group, end of 16th century)
      1957 Kühnel p. 11 (problem of origin still open; possibly Qazvin; towards end of 16th century)
      1958 Bode/Kühnel: ('closely related to that medallion group which tentatively has been traced back to Qazvin . . . end of the 16th century' (a reference to the article on the Cassirer carpet by Kühnel, 1957))
      1964 Ellis: copy of a Kashan but from Northwest Persia (see Beattie, Leeds, 1964 (20))
      1964 Spuhler p. 594
Exh: 1914 London (29) Pl. 7 (Persian 17th century)
      1931 London (125) (late 16th century)
      1956 Rome, Mostra d'Arte Iranica (587)
      1964 Leeds (20) (Persian 16th or 17th century)

8

The Figdor Silk Kilim. A multiple-medallion design of alternately reversed shield-shaped forms, alternating with rows of cartouches and quatrefoils, decorates a deep ivory field. Medallions as well as the intervening spaces contain animals or birds. Broad S-stems with an arabesque at one end, another on the diagonal and cartouches containing birds on the conjunctions of the stems, form the design on the sky-blue border, between red and orange guards.

Silk tapestry-woven carpet enriched with metal-wrapped silk, late 16th century.
Width: 125 cm (4 ft 1 in)
Length: 192 cm (6 ft 4 in)

Thyssen-Bornemisza Collection, Lugano, Switzerland, Inv. No. 669.

This carpet, which is one of the group of kilims with animal designs, exemplifies the beauty of silk tapestry-woven rugs of Court quality towards the end of the sixteenth century. The colours are still most attractive but they have been much softened by time and are not nearly as brilliant as they once were.

8

Erdmann compared the design with that of the woollen-pile Multiple-medallion carpet (no. 7, Plate 4). In both, the forms represented in the medallions, and in the background, are arranged directionally throughout, although the kilim medallions are inverted at one end.

Only two other rugs in this style are known. One published in 1938[1] has not been heard of since; the other, in Japan, is said to have been the favourite campaigning coat of Toyotomi Hideyoshi[2] who died in 1598.

[1] Robinson p. 102
[2] Kodama p. 80

Coll: Dr Albert Figdor, Vienna
Lit: 1910 Sarre p. 478 Ill. 15 (Persian beginning 17th century)
1912 Sarre & Martin p. iv Pl. 63 (Persian 16th–17th century)
1930 Orendi p. 205 264 Ill. 967 (Persian c.1650)
1931 Erdmann p. 659f. (Central Persian 17th century)
1939 Surv. p. 2404 Pl. 1268A (Kashan early 17th century)
1941 Erdmann p. 170 (Kashan early 17th, late 16th century)
1968a Spuhler pp. 125, 246, W.26 (Kashan c.1600)
1972 Beattie p. 31f. (Kashan late 16th century)

Note: for a more extensive list of the references to this carpet see Beattie 1972
Exh: 1910 Munich (86) (Persia 17th century)
1930 Munich (79) ('Josbagan Ghali bei Isfahan' c.1600)
1931 London (369) (E. Persia c.1600)
1936 Zurich (p. 48f.) ('Josbagan Ghali bei Isfahan' c.1600)

9

Border design of octafoils and lobed lozenges, linked transversely and longitudinally by small roundels, and diagonally by small cartouches, on a red background. Remains of a blue field with multiple medallions and floral motifs.

Woollen-pile carpet fragment, second half 17th century.
Width: 65 cm (2 ft 1½ in)
Length: 280 cm (9 ft 2½ in)

Firma Bernheimer, Munich, Inv. 51255.

The only other border design of this type known to me is that of the famous Multiple-medallion carpet in Sarajevo which is dated 1656,[1] but in that carpet the background of the border is yellow. Here the original colour is modified by overpainting.

It is not now possible to say what the field design of this carpet was, other than that it had multiple medallions with strap-like outlines reminiscent of those in no. 7. Cloud bands, as opposed to small coiled forms, are not common in 'Vase'-technique rugs but they are used in the field of the Sarajevo carpet and also here, in a lobed lozenge in the border.

Technical notes on this fragment mention the cotton wefts as being mainly 'drab', a term which also applies to those of the Sarajevo carpet and that in the Victoria and Albert Museum (see no. 52). Regrettably no part of the former is available for comparison.

[1] Surv. Pl. 1238

Lit: 1959 Bernheimer Ill. 59 (Isfahan fragment – South Persia c.1600)

9

10

offset rows of little scenes used in the manner of a textile repeat. From the structure of this, which I noticed first in 1965, and of the Munich piece, I would not expect the carpet to have been woven in Tabriz or even in Northwest Persia.

A directional design of animals and cypresses used, as here, like a textile repeat, also occurs in a silk-pile carpet in Munich.[1]

[1] Surv. Pl. 1251

Coll: Bacher
Lit: 1942 Erdmann p. 407
     1953 Erdmann col. 204 (North Persia)
     1968 Beattie p. 5 (Kirman)
Exh: 1950 Hamburg (102) (North Persia (Tabriz?) 17th century)
     1971 Hamburg–Frankfurt p. 48 (exhibited in Frankfurt but not listed)

11

10

Directional design of animals and trees on a deep blue field, with a red and yellow chevron inner guard and remains of a red border main stripe with floral design.

Woollen-pile carpet fragment, 17th century.
Width: 63 cm (2 ft 1 in)
Length: 145 cm (4 ft 9 in)

Museum für Kunsthandwerk, Frankfurt-am-Main, Inv. 4737 (acquired 1908 from private possession).

This is the upper left corner from the same carpet as no. 11. The design is orientated in the same direction and is unlikely ever to have had a medallion. It is simpler than the ascending designs of the Sanguszko carpets in Paris (no. 68) and East Berlin (no. 69) and to judge from the three known fragments consisted of

II

Directional design of animals and trees on a deep blue field with a red and yellow chevron guard.

Woollen-pile carpet fragment, 17th century.
Width: 75 cm (2 ft 6 in)
Length: 109 cm (3 ft 7 in)

Firma Bernheimer, Munich, Inv. 63–51182.

This is the lower right corner of a carpet (see no. 10). The little animal (lower left) beside the willow, cypress and flowering tree is reversed and used further up on the right side of a smaller fragment, once in the Baranovicz Collection. By analogy the one here should be completed with a long, slightly raised tail. In 1942 Erdmann 'considered the design to be a descendant of the Williams Tree carpet',[1] but in 1950 associated it with the medallion designs with paired cypresses such as the Hermitage fragment (no. 1a). He assigned it to North Persia, and this provenance has been repeated in later catalogues. He also pointed to the use of closely related designs in later rugs from the Persian-Caucasian border region.

[1] Surv. Pl. 1126

Lit: 1942 Erdmann p. 407 Ill. 3 (North Persia 17th century)
1953 Erdmann col. 204 (North Persian)
1959 Bernheimer Ill. 63 (Isfahan–South Persia 17th–18th century)
1968 Beattie p. 5 (Kirman)
1974 Beattie p. 449
Exh: 1950 Hamburg (101) Ill. 38 (North Persia (Tabriz?) 17th century)
1971 Hamburg-Frankfurt (17) (North Persia (Tabriz))

12

Directional design of naturalistic plants in offset rows on a blue ground, with small superimposed medallion and cornerpieces. The red border has areas of pink between adjoining pairs of alternately reversed arabesques. Reciprocal-trefoil guards are ivory and blue, and yellow and red to brownish purple.

Woollen-pile carpet, 17th century.
Width: 183 cm (6 ft)
Length: 402 cm (13 ft 2 in)

Textile Museum, Washington, D.C., Inv. R 33.3.4.

The design exemplifies flowering plants and trees in a more naturalistic style than is usual in more numerous pieces where they have stiffened to somewhat rigid forms (no. 13 Plate 5). Such designs were extremely popular in Mughal carpets, especially in the time of Shāh Jahān. The medallion in the centre

of the carpet has been replaced but traces of the original remain. The cornerpieces relate the carpet to some with arabesque designs (cf. no. 28, Plate 7).

This particular border shows how colour can be used to create special effects. When paired arabesques in a simple undecorated form are alternately reversed and arranged on a single colour as in no. 32 (Plate 8), an attractive border results, but when, as here, a contrasting colour is introduced into the spaces between adjoining arabesques of different pairs, a completely different effect is produced.

This style of border with colour change characterized a three-plane lattice design in a rug exhibited by W. Ginzkey in Vienna in 1891[1] and is the type referred to, for convenience, as a 'Ginzkey' border. A rug formerly in the Dumbarton Oaks Collection had a similar border (see no. 58) and an attractive fragment[2] is in the Musée des Tissus in Lyons.

Further variety results when two colours alternate in the spaces between adjoining arabesques as in a fragment in the Hermitage and in another, known only from a photograph. A rug in Sarajevo provides a third variation where the terminal leaflets of the two little stems, which rise from the tip of each border palmette, are increased in length and overlap the adjoining arabesques. Alternate spaces so enclosed contain contrasting colours.

These borders are largely associated with three-plane lattice designs, either with floral scrolls or with flowering-plant backgrounds, so that it is not surprising to find one combined, as here, with a straightforward flowering-plant field design.

In 1925 Riefstahl[3] discussed the 'Ginzkey' border as a curvilinear version of the rectilinear 'bird' motif of the sixteenth–seventeenth century white-ground Anatolian carpets.

[1] Clarke Pl. LXVIII
[2] Inv. 30.417
[3] p. 93

Coll: J.P. Morgan
Joseph V. McMullan
Lit: 1965 McMullan Pl. 18 (Vase carpet variant; School of Shāh 'Abbās)
1968 Ellis p. 28 Fig. 13 (Kirman)
Exh: 1970 New York (60) (Kirman? early 17th century)
1972 London (18)

12

13

13 (Colour Plate 5)

Directional design of stylized flowering plants in offset rows on a blue-green field. The red border main stripe with alternately reversed pairs of arabesques on a floral scroll background lies between ivory, and deep-blue and ivory reciprocal 'heart', guards.

Woollen-pile carpet fragment, 17th century.
Width: 64 cm (2 ft 1 in)
Length: 126 cm (4 ft 1½ in)

Textile Museum, Washington, D.C., Inv. R 33.3.2.

The flowering plants in this design are bilaterally symmetrical and the pairs of stems are of such a length that the contour of each motif forms a smooth curve. They begin to approximate to the 'boteh' or 'leaf' form which in Kashmir and, in due course, in Paisley shawls evolves from the flowering plants used in seventeenth-century Indian textile designs.[1] The motif was widespread in Persian carpets in the nineteenth century and is still popular.

This stylized form of the design, but on a red field, occurs on a similar fragment in Brooklyn Museum[2] and on rusty orange on a large carpet somewhat reduced in length in Tryon Palace, New Bern.[3] A small fragment was in the Baranovicz Collection. Others, variously stylized, are in the Metropolitan Museum,[4] the Philadelphia Museum of Art[5] and Newark Museum,[6] U.S.A.

[1] Irwin pp. 11ff.
[2] Inv. 46.189.34
[3] Inv. 61–25
[4] Surv. Pl. 1231
[5] Inv. 1968–8–28
[6] Inv. 49.539

Lit:　1968　Ellis p. 28 Fig. 12 (Kirman)

14

Directional design of flowering plants alternating with cypresses in offset rows on a rusty orange field. The deep blue border main stripe has alternately reversed palmettes separated by wiry stems ending in outswept leaves, between light yellow and greenish-blue guards.

Woollen-pile carpet fragment, 17th–18th century.
Width: 119 cm (3 ft 11 in)
Length: 406 cm (13 ft 4 in)

Victoria and Albert Museum, London, Inv. 3–1887.

To judge from an end fragment with a border and one row of motifs, in the Beshar Collection in New York, which is probably from the same rug, this design originally contained four complete and two halved cypresses in alternate rows. Both pieces have the same little monochrome 'clouds' which occur in so many of the rugs, and also an unusual border.

The closely related carpet with a similar rusty orange field, but without cypresses, in Tryon Palace, New Bern, mentioned in no. 13 has a yellow and blue arabesque border between floral guards. Flowering trees alternating with cypresses also occur in borders, especially of rather late rugs, such as one with a three-plane lattice design formerly in the Bruce and Kolkhorst Collections[1] and in no. 56. In a fragment in the Hermitage[2] the cypresses overlap the flowering trees.

This long fragment, of which only a detail is reproduced here, was published by Martin in 1908, in the book which contributed so much information about the provenance of antique rugs. Much of what he said is still of value but his dating is not now always accepted.

[1] Schurmann 35
[2] Inv. V.T. 1063

Lit:　1908　Martin p. 87 Fig. 185 (Kirman c. 1520)

14

15 (Colour Plate 6)

The Corcoran Throne Rug. A sickle-leaf design with spiralling stems, palmettes and long curved leaves on a background of various trees, has quartered small medallions superimposed on the corners at the beginning of the rug (by weave), and three halved medallions at the ending. Overlapping S-stems on the deep blue border terminate in sprays of flowers, which swing around diagonal palmettes.

Woollen-pile carpet, Shāh ʿAbbās period.
Width: 195 cm (6 ft 5 in)
Length: 265 cm (8 ft 8½ in)

Corcoran Gallery of Art, William A. Clark Collection (on loan to the Textile Museum, Washington), Inv. 26–278.

This is one of the most beautifully drawn and elegant of the many 'Vase'-technique carpets. Like the formal Garden carpet designs it can be regarded as a bird's eye view of a woody landscape, here seen through festoons of spiralling creepers terminating in slender sickle leaves, and bearing the large floral motifs familiar in so many of the lattice designs. The pairs of such motifs, which lie transversely and are directed alternately medially and latterally, suggest influences from eastern Persia.

It is customary to hang rugs in such a way that the velvety pile can be smoothed downwards without resistance in the direction of that part of the rug which was first woven. This practice has not been followed here, as it is more pleasant to contemplate supine deciduous trees, perhaps bent over by the wind, than to look at cypresses apparently balancing on their tips. Two-way 'movements' in design which are equally pleasant viewed from either end are common, especially in three-plane lattice carpets (p. 26), but here the rug is best viewed from the three halved medallions. Like the Wagner carpet (no. 1, Plate 1) and a Polonaise in Hanover,[1] the Corcoran rug has no doubt been woven from a half cartoon which, in its entirety, would have the three medallions in the centre of the field. Pope suggested that the proportions indicated its use on a throne dais from which, presumably, is derived the name, the 'Corcoran Throne Rug.'

[1] Bode/Kühnel 1958 No. 111

Lit:	1939	Surv. p. 2384f. Pl. 1234 (Joshagan Gali or Isfahan period of Shāh ʿAbbās I)
	1941	Erdmann pp. 174 178f 186 188
	1960	Erdmann No. 85 (Kirman first half 17th century)
	1963	Schlosser No. 53 (Persian Court first half 17th century)
	1968	Ellis p. 19 Fig. 2 (Kirman mid-16th century)
	1973	Dimand/Mailey Fig. 107 (probably Kirman early 17th century)
Exh:	1972	Washington (6) (South Persia 17th century)
	1973	New York (30) (17th century)
	1974	Fogg Art Museum, Cambridge, Mass.

15

16

Sickle-leaf and flowering-plant design on a deep blue field, with remains of a red floral border.

Woollen-pile carpet fragment, 17th century.
Width: 104 cm (3 ft 4 in)
Length: 253 cm (8 ft 3 in)

Textile Museum, Washington, D.C., Inv. R 33.6.6.

The sickle leaves, the large motifs on the stems, and the plants in opposed directions, relate this rug distantly to the Corcoran Throne Rug, but the weaver has had difficulty in executing motifs which should be diagonally placed, or at least has misunderstood them, as one would expect in a rug woven after the peak period of the design had passed. A larger section might have shown that the design was better balanced than appears from this fragment.

The arrangement of a small animal with a large vine-leaf palmette in its mouth has a parallel in another little creature, also with a large leaf, in the pendants of the Getty Medallion-and-landscape carpet.[1]

The remarkably beautiful colouring of these rugs is again obvious in this example.

16

[1] Surv. Pl. 1128

Lit: 1931 Magazine of Art (May)
       1939 Surv. p. 2451 note 3
       1968 Ellis p. 29 Fig. 16 (Kirman)
Exh: 1931 London (842) (Safavid 16th century)
       1951 Pottstown, Pa., The Hill School

17

Sickle-leaf design of long serrated leaves and palmettes borne on heavily veined stems, arranged over scrolling vines against a red background.

Woollen-pile carpet fragments, 17th century.
a)
Width: 124 cm (4 ft)
Length: 78 cm (2 ft 6 in)
b)
Width: 24 cm ($9\frac{1}{2}$ in)
Length: 44 cm (1 ft 5 in)

Staatl. Museum für Völkerkunde, Munich, Inv. 14–47–30, 31.

These two fragments give a slight idea of a handsome but uncertain design, which at this point would appear to be continuous if the missing area between the fragments were replaced; but the colour of certain details disproves this and the two pieces must come from more widely separated parts of the carpet. One fragment of similar style, formerly in the Baranovicz Collection, and another[1] (much pieced) in Lyons, are notable for a large, almost distorted, field motif with falls like an iris and curled 'standards' rising from the centre. The latter still has a stretch of border the same in design but rather more graceful than that of the Gulbenkian blue-ground Sickle-leaf carpet (no. 70); and the same border type characterizes a piece once in the Ghernon[2] and Perez Collections.[3] Of two other fragments with graceful sickle leaves on red fields, one is in the Boston Museum of Fine Arts[4] and the other was in the Erlenmeyer Collection. A third piece, formerly in the Baranovicz Collection, is said to have a brownish-yellow field. The graceful drawing, the variety of colours and the survival of numerous fragments, all point to the one-time popularity of this type of design.

[1] Inv. 30–858
[2] Tav. xv Sale cat. 1934
[3] No. 0.6522
[4] Inv. 04–1698

Lit: 1916/17 Münch. Jahrb. p. 292 Ill. 21
      1942   Erdmann p. 403
Exh: 1963   Munich (328)

17

18

Sickle-leaf design with veined 'bract' stems bearing large floral motifs and brilliantly coloured serrated leaves, which are arranged against a background of flowering trees and cypresses on a deep blue field. Traces of a red and yellow reciprocal-V inner guard remain.

Woollen-pile carpet fragment, 17th century.
Width: 63.5 cm (2 ft 1½ in)
Length: 131.5 cm (4 ft 4 in)

Burrell Collection, Glasgow Art Gallery and Museum, Inv. 9–15.

The fragment is from the upper left corner of the carpet. The fact that the large yellow sickle leaf terminates a stem shows that this is not one of the three-plane lattice designs in which such a motif, usually overlying a rosette, would be used in the same way as a vase or a palmette, on a lattice stem which follows an undulating course along the field. The landscape background with cypresses is more usual in designs without such stems. The leaves are broader, more serrated and less graceful than in the Corcoran Throne rug and could well be the prototype for those used in some of the handsome 'Kuba' rugs of the Caucasus.[1] Their size and brilliance of colour make them an outstanding feature of the design, and the multicoloured segmented form calls to mind a similar arrangement in Mughal rugs.

[1] Ellis 1975 Pl. 22

Lit: 1968   Ellis p. 29 note 96 (Kirman)
       1975   Ellis Fig. 11 (Kirman)

19

Sickle-leaf design with veined bract-stems. S-stems terminating in bicoloured leaves with rosettes and alternately reversed lotus palmettes decorate the red main stripe of the border. Reciprocal-V guard.

Woollen-pile carpet fragment, 17th century.
Width: 73.5 cm (2 ft 5 in)
Length: 143.5 cm (4 ft 10 in)

Victoria and Albert Museum, London, Inv. 360–1892.

As this fragment is from the upper right corner of, presumably, the same carpet as no. 18 and includes some of the border, the two pieces taken together give an idea of a splendid and colourful design apparently unknown in any complete carpet woven in the 'vase'-technique. Although different in design the monumental style is in the manner of no. 17.

18

19

20

Sickle-leaf design of heavily veined stems, floral motifs and coiled 'clouds' with a background of flowering vines, on a dark blue field. The stems on the red main stripe of the border bear rosettes and sickle leaves but their arrangement is uncertain.

Woollen-pile carpet, 17th century.
Width: 65 cm (2 ft 1 in)
Length: 25 cm (9⅞ in)

Textile Museum, Washington, D.C., Inv. 1968–11–6.

This is another example of a sickle-leaf design with heavily veined primary stems, but with a background of fine stems instead of the landscape style with flowering trees as in the two previous examples. In common with them it has the reciprocal-V guard, but a somewhat different border design. A corner fragment with border and details similar to this, possibly from the same rug, was in the Kelekian Collection[1] and four small fragments[2] lacking the border main stripe but alike in guard and colouring are in the Victoria and Albert Museum. In 1970 the Erlenmeyer Collection contained several other pieces apparently from one rug which had yet another border design with a plain yellow inner line instead of the reciprocal-V guard. The survival of fragments from several different rugs points to a large production of the type.

[1] Migeon 1909 Pl. 2
[2] T. 369–1966

21

Sickle-leaf and medallion design in which an eight-pointed wine-red lobed medallion on a blue field is superimposed on fine undulating stems, from which sickle leaves sweep out rhythmically around large floral motifs. The design of the border main stripe is of deep blue strap-like arabesques on red, between yellow and blue guards.

Woollen-pile carpet fragment, 17th century.
Width: 114 cm (3 ft 9 in)
Length: 280 cm (9 ft 2 in)

Musée du Louvre, Paris (gift of the heirs of Jacques Acheroff 1974), Inv. MAO–491–F.

21

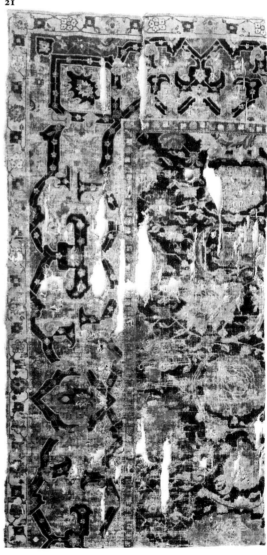

20

Worn as this fragment is, it further enlarges our knowledge of sickle-leaf designs. The superimposition of a large central medallion (not shown in the illustration) on such a field design appears to be unique. The gradation of colours from dark blue through light blue to ivory-yellow in the border arabesques is an arrangement familiar in the well-known 'Portuguese' carpets[1] as well as in many Chinese rugs. Erdmann[2] discussed the relationship of potentially extensible border designs of this type to field patterns. He assumed that the lozenges in the border of the Berlin 'Portuguese' carpet, now destroyed, were misunderstood arabesque arrangements. Here such a derivation certainly looks possible, but the designs of 'Vase'-technique rugs often contain lozenges. A small fragment of this type was in the Baranovicz Collection and Martin[3] illustrates a stretch of border in the same design which he attributes to Shiraz, about 1680.

[1] Surv. Pls. 1215–17
[2] 1961 p. 156
[3] Fig. 181

Coll: Acheroff

22

Sickle-leaf design of long, slim, bicoloured leaves which sweep around large palmettes, against a background of angular floral stems on a deep blue field. The large, red, orange and white pairs of sickle leaves enclose cypresses flanked by flowering trees, on the dark blue border. Part of a yellow and red reciprocal-trefoil outer guard and an inner pink line remain.

Woollen-pile carpet fragments, late 17th century.
Width: 132.5 cm (4 ft 4 in)
Length: 190 cm (6 ft 3 in)

Textile Museum, Washington, D.C., Inv. R. 33–6–8.

It is exceptional among antique rugs, particularly of this group, to find a piece so provincial in drawing. It shows the inclination of an unsupervised weaver to use straight lines and angles rather than smooth curves. Excellence of drawing, or the absence of it, is not necessarily an indication of date, but misunderstanding of a once well-constructed design is. Here not only is the drawing provincial and the weaving of a diagonally placed vine-leaf palmette beyond the skill of the weaver, but the stems fail to follow the expected course. Caucasian weavers, in particular, adopted the border design and used it

22

in their eighteenth- and nineteenth-century carpets.

Although this fragment is both provincial and late it has a wealth of beautiful colour typical of rugs in the 'vase'-technique.

Another fragment, once in the Baranovicz Collection, shows clearly that the outer guard consisted of reciprocal trefoils.

Lit: 1968   Ellis p. 29 Fig. 15
        1970   Ellis p. 204 Fig. 9

23

Arabesque and animal design on a deep blue field. The yellow border has red S-stems terminating in blue 'silhouette' lilies.

Woollen-pile carpet fragment, 17th century.
Width: 23 cm (9 in)
Length: 84 cm (2 ft 9 in)

Staatl. Museum für Völkerkunde, Munich, Inv. 32–50–18.

In 1942 Erdmann pointed out that this fragment represented a hitherto unknown type of design. Small as it is, it is still of sufficient size to show the existence of a strap-like arabesque and veined stem design on a blue ground, which in its present state justifies classifying it with the red ground Metropolitan Museum Arabesque and Animal carpet (no. 71).

The fragment has a complex design with true medallions properly superimposed on the veined and strap-like stems. One medallion contains a little blue cervid, the other a lion. Both these animals have counterparts in Dragon carpets of the Caucasus. The border design is that used in a Dragon carpet which was probably the prototype for so many forgeries of that type of rug.

Lit: 1942   Erdmann p. 403; 1975 Ellis Fig. 4
               (Kirman)
Exh: 1963   Munich (327)

24 (see front cover)

Arabesque, animal and sickle-leaf border design with a reciprocal-V guard. Thin, deep blue, undulating stems bearing large rosettes and palmettes with green floral scrolls are arranged on a dull pink field.

Woollen-pile carpet fragment, 17th century.
Width: 143 cm (4 ft 8 in)
Length: 141 cm (4 ft 7½ in)

Musée des Tissus, Lyons, Inv. 31.091.

The important feature of this fragment is the border, which could easily be extended in width and length to form a handsome field pattern. It thus provides yet another example of an arabesque and animal design, here combined with large sickle leaves, and it relates several motifs, each of which may be the outstanding form in other designs. The dull pink of the field exemplifies one of the rather unusual shades used in these rugs, but the purple patch in one corner is probably another part of no. 41 which is in the same collection. If, as Erdmann suggests, the Sanguszko animal carpets come from Kashan, and the Vase carpets, which are largely devoid of animals, come from Kirman, one cannot help wondering what provenance he would have suggested for no. 23 which he referred to as unique, for this fragment with an animal border and a field somewhat similar to the Vase carpets, and for the Metropolitan Museum carpet (no. 71) recently referred to as 'probably Kurdistan'.

The field somewhat resembles the three-plane lattice design (p. 26) but it is an aberrant form not truly characteristic of that type, and, unfortunately, insufficient of the rug remains to trace the course of the stems. In comparison with the border, the field design is weak. Possibly a central medallion once existed which would have counteracted that impression.

24

Inversion of the fragment displays the design most pleasingly, although, as woven, the large ivory vine-leaf palmette containing the red ibex should be in the lower right corner. The red vine leaf cut off by the end border contains part of a spotted yellow fish. Paired fish are not unusual in 'Vase'-technique rugs (see nos. 1a, 3, 64 and 65) and Kühnel[1] illustrated a series of such motifs when discussing the Berlin Cassirer carpet (no. 64). Robinson[2] drew attention to a slightly different form in a little-known silk kilim of the same type as no. 8.

[1] 1957 p. 8f.
[2] 1938 p. 104f.

25

25

Arabesque and floral design on a purple field. The yellow main stripe of the border, with its large leaves and floral motifs, lies between S-stem guards.

Woollen-pile carpet fragment, 17th century.
Width: 38 cm (1 ft 3 in)
Length: 80 cm (2 ft 7½ in)

Staatl. Museum für Völkerkunde, Munich, Inv. 14.47.33.

Although so little remains it is evident from the gracefulness of the drawing and the elegance of the motifs that this was part of another magnificent carpet. The trefoil-like motif in one corner and that cut by the border are similar to such motifs in the Corcoran Throne Rug (no. 15, Plate 6) and the little animal fragment (no. 23) from Munich.

The combination of complementary colours – a purple field and a yellow border – can hardly be imagined in any other group of rugs. Whether or not the increased use of purples, browns and yellows in Persian miniature paintings from about 1625 to 1635[1] influenced the colours used in carpets is not known. Certainly the dyers who prepared the yarns for this group of rugs had the knowledge and the skill, more so perhaps than had such craftsmen elsewhere, to follow contemporary fashion in colour.

[1] Kendal exhibition 1967

26

Arabesque design on a red field, with blue-green and plum-coloured simulated medallions and floral scrolls.

Woollen-pile carpet fragment, 17th century.
Width: 40 cm (15¼ in)
Length: 93 cm (37 in)

Museum of Fine Arts, Boston (gift of Miss Betty Prather, 1932), Inv. 32–90.

This and the following fragment (no. 27) appear to be parts of one carpet. Martin[1] illustrated a larger piece with a blue border which until recently was in the Baranovicz Collection. He regarded it as Kirman about 1520, a date which would not be acceptable today. Pairs of arabesques rising from alternately reversed palmettes, the red directed medially, the green laterally, decorated the main stripe of the border, and a meandering vine, from which drooped small flowers, the inner guard. Jacoby[2] reconstructed a still larger section which he illustrated in colour, and other fragments may have existed from which he took the design for the border corner and outer guard.

The elegant curves of this fragment and the open uncrowded style are notable. A fragment of a shaped carpet (no. 73) also in Boston, which unfortunately by the terms of the bequest is not available for the exhibition, a magnificent long multiple medallion and arabesque strip[3] in Sarajevo and a border illustrated by Martin[4] give a similar impression.

[1] p. 77 Fig. 188
[2] 1952 frontispiece
[3] Clarke Pl. xxxix
[4] Pl. xx, No. 4

Coll: Miss Betty Prather

26

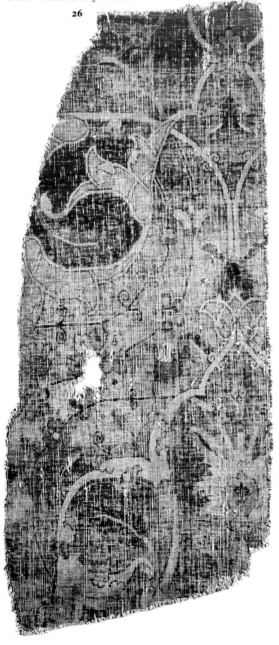

27

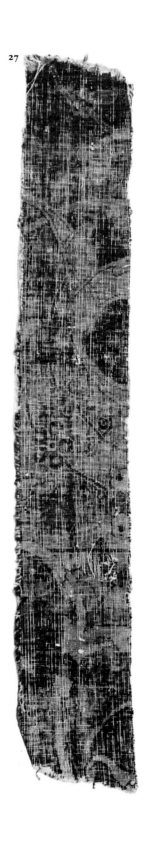

27

Arabesque design as for no. 26.

Woollen-pile carpet, 17th century.
Width: 14 cm (5½ in)
Length: 90 cm (33½ in)

Musée du Louvre, Paris (gift of the heirs of Jacques Acheroff, 1974), Inv. MAO–491–E.

From photographs the design of this piece is continuous with that of no. 26, but the two will need to be seen together to judge if the colours are the same.

Coll: Acheroff

28 (Colour Plate 7)

Arabesque design with medallion and cornerpieces with a background of floral scrolls on a light yellow field. Rusty orange and light blue interlaced arabesques, scrolling vines and little rosettes, decorate the bluish-purple border stripe between ivory and reciprocal red and blue guards.

Woollen-pile carpet, 17th century.
Width: 284.5 cm (9 ft 4 in)
Length: 348 cm (11 ft 5 in)

Burrell Collection, Glasgow Art Gallery and Museum, Inv. 9–3.

The design of blue and red arabesques is balanced in both directions; and, in four places, four diagonally arranged arabesques form an inconspicuous lozenge-motif that is familiar, in rectilinear drawing, in many Anatolian rugs. The superimposed medallion and precise quarters of medallions in the corners suggest a centralized design, but the five offset rows of medallions in an arabesque carpet in the Deering Collection[1] make it much more likely that the medallion arrangement here is simply a small section of a potentially extensible repeat superimposed on an arabesque design, and so two types of repeat design are combined to create variety.

[1] Surv. Pl. 1239

Lit: 1961   Beattie p. 5 Fig. 4
        1968b Spuhler p. 64f. Ill. 1
Exh: 1949   Glasgow (802)
        1951   Glasgow (33)
        1969   Glasgow (1)
        1975   London (284) (Safavid 16th century)

29

Arabesque and vase design with a background of floral scrolls on a red field. The blue border stripe bears continuous pairs of arabesques, the red directed medially, the pink laterally, on floral scrolls. Ivory and yellow guards both with S stems.

Woollen-pile carpet, late 17th century.
Width: 178 cm (5 ft 10 in)
Length: 271 cm (8 ft 10½ in)

Firma Bernheimer, Munich, Inv. 46–242.

Vases arranged in obvious rows are exceptional in 'Vase'-technique rugs. Here, in a design balanced in both directions, they are linked by systematically arranged branching stems bearing arabesques and palmettes, the latter mainly where the stems come in contact. The drawing of the arabesques and stems and the shape of the brackets bearing the vases and the palmettes in the border all give a late impression. A similar piece was in the London trade in 1964.

Exh: 1934   Basle (92)
       1950   Hamburg (79) Ill. 29 (Kirman 17th century)
       1971   Hamburg–Frankfurt (20) (Kirman 17th century late)

30

30

Arabesque, medallion and corner design with quarters of green medallions of two types on a blue field; red arabesque stems as well as background scrolls bear large floral motifs. Continuous pairs of slim arabesques, the green directed laterally, the blue medially, alternate on the red border, between multicolour chevron and reciprocal-trefoil guards.

Woollen-pile carpet fragments, 17th century.
Width: 141 cm (4 ft 7½ in)
Length: 207 cm (6 ft 9½ in)

Metropolitan Museum of Art, New York, Inv. 1970–302–4.

If these fragments are all from one carpet, it must originally have been over twenty feet in length, as the direction of the weave shows. The superimposed design may therefore have consisted of an offset arrangement of two medallion types. The background scrolls tend to break into sprays of flowers influenced no doubt by the fashion for flowering plants. This tendency is also apparent in no. 28.

The rug is unusual on three counts. Both the primary arabesques and the fine background scrolls of the field bear the type of large motif – such as palmette, rosette and vase-on-bracket – which is used so frequently in the three- and two-plane lattice designs formed of undulating stems (p. 26). To judge from similar fragments,[1] which may or may not be part of this rug, the design may also contain irises and coiled 'clouds'. This type of design therefore links the arabesque and lattice styles. A second unusual feature is the type of border – arabesques drawn in a graceful but severe style distinctly different from other examples in this section; and thirdly, the chevron design of the outer guard (cf. no. 56) when arranged as parallel stripes occurs in medallion-like motifs in several rugs such as no. 47 and as a filler in lattice spaces.[2] Martin[3] illustrates another but less graceful example of such a design with a heavy arabesque border as in nos. 45 and 46. He regarded it as South Persian, about 1600.

[1] McMullan 20; V&A Inv. 1825–1888
[2] Kühnel 1930 p. 461
[3] Pl. xix

Lit: 1965   McMullan No. 21 (Persian rug, School of Shāh 'Abbās)
       1968b   Spuhler p. 62f.
       1970   Spuhler p. 144
Exh: 1968–9   Frankfurt (12) (Isfahan c. 1600)

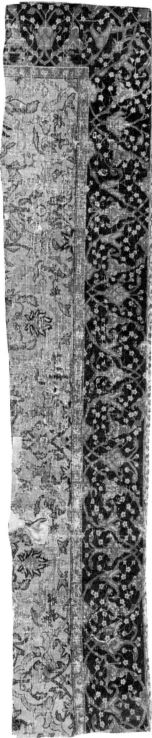

Arabesque design of lozenges in offset arrangement linked by blue leafy stems, on an ochre field. Pairs of alternately reversed red and blue arabesques, on a background of delicate scrolling stems with numerous little blossoms, decorate the blue border. Pale yellow and red guards.

Woollen-pile carpet, 17th century.
Width: 66 cm (2 ft 2 in)
Length: 295 cm (9 ft 8 in)

Keir Collection.

The nature of the field design, unique in 'Vase'-technique rugs, would be uncertain were it not for a fairly large, pieced and worn example[1] in the Hermitage Museum in Leningrad, quite possibly from the same carpet. It has offset rows of pink arabesques arranged in lozenges of two types. In one, those arabesques which join on the horizontal line are directed inwards, as in no. 26. In the other the four arabesques are diagonally placed. A similar rectilinear form is the secondary motif of the Anatolian Holbein design characterized by primary interlace-edged octagons.

The arrangement of this design is reminiscent of the small repetitive patterns depicted in carpets in miniatures prior to the marked change in style towards the end of the fifteenth century, and may therefore represent a continuance of the old tradition in a curvilinear and floral style. The border is one of the most attractive of the slim arabesque designs and, here, is particularly rich in little rosettes.

[1] Inv. V.T. 999

Coll: Erlenmeyer, Basle
Lit: 1972 Sotheby (18) (Herat late 17th century)

32 (Colour Plate 8)
Arabesque and flowering plant design in which red and yellow arabesques divide, join and interlace on a sky-blue field, against a background of flowering plants. Pairs of arabesques, sand-coloured directed laterally, and blue medially, are arranged on a red border with a red and yellow reciprocal inner guard.

Woollen-pile carpet fragment, second quarter 17th century.
Width: 75 cm (2 ft 5½ in)
Length: 122 cm (4 ft)
Firma Bernheimer, Munich, Inv. 63–51183.

This is one of the most attractive of the arabesque designs, possibly because a subsidiary design of flowering plants rather than floral scrolls requires more extended and graceful arabesques to provide adequate space for the plants.

The attractive shade of blue used in the field also occurs in a closely related fragment[1] in Vienna which has a similar but more complex border in the manner of no. 31.

Such designs on yellow fields are in the Burrell[2] and formerly in the Kann Collection.[3] The border design of the former consists of arabesques devoid of floral scrolls; that of the latter has rather heavy arabesques and palmettes.

A large carpet[4] in the Metropolitan Museum provides a close link between the Arabesque and Lattice carpets. The design begins with blue and yellow arabesques on a flowering plant background and after a short distance switches abruptly to a three-plane lattice design on a floral scroll background, obvious evidence that such types were woven contemporaneously and in the same place.

[1] Sarre & Trenkwald I Pl. 31
[2] Inv. 9–4
[3] No. 504
[4] Surv. Pl. 1219

32

Lit: 1929   Sarre & Trenkwald II Pl. 8
      1959   Bernheimer Fig. 61 (Kirman–South Persian end 16th century)
Exh: 1926   Chicago (21) (Joshagan early 17th century)
      1950   Hamburg (77) Ill. 25 (Kirman end 16th century)
      1971   Hamburg and Frankfurt (6) (Kirman end 16th century)

33

Three-plane lattice design with a background of floral scrolls on a deep blue field. Overlapping S-stems terminating in floral sprays, palmettes and rosettes decorate the light orange border.

Woollen-pile carpet fragment, Shāh ʿAbbās period.
Width: 116 cm (3 ft 9½ in)
Length: 258 cm (8 ft 5½ in)

Textile Museum, Washington, D.C., Inv. R 33.6.5.

For long there has been discussion as to whether the Berlin fragment no. 34 and certain other pieces are all parts of one carpet. The exhibited fragment from the Textile Museum is from the upper left corner of a rug and because of its similarity in colour, and the fact that parts of motifs which have been cut through correspond with others in a fragment[1] from the right side in the Arab Museum in Cairo, both pieces must be from one carpet. The Cairo fragment lacks a stretch of field next to the upper border. Wiet regarded it as sixteenth–seventeenth century. Since pairs of rugs in the same design are not unusual, the question remained as to whether those two were parts of the Berlin rug. The opportunity to compare this and the Berlin fragment is welcomed (see no. 35).

[1] Inv. 3607 Wiet 1933 Pl. XLIV

Coll: Lamm, Sweden
Lit: 1908   Martin p. 78 Pl. XVI (Southern Persia c.1520)
      1968   Ellis p. 19 Fig. 1 (Kirman mid-16th century)
      1975   Ellis Fig. 20 (early Kirman vase rug)

34 (Colour Plate 9)

Three-plane lattice design with a background of floral scrolls on a deep blue field. Overlapping S-stems terminating in graceful floral sprays, with palmettes and rosettes decorate the pale orange border.

Woollen-pile carpet fragment, Shāh ʿAbbās period.
Width: 144 cm (4 ft 8½ in)
Length: 244–9 cm (8 ft–8 ft 2 in)

Museum für Islamische Kunst, Stiftung Preussischer Kulturbesitz, Berlin, Federal Republic of Germany, Inv. I–8–72.

points to the work of meticulous craftsmen who may well have been employed in a workshop directly patronized by the Court.

This style of border with sprays of flowers can hardly be other than the prototype for the 'frozen' forms of later rugs,[1] which must result from mechanical repetition of a familiar form.

[1] See Ellis 1968 p. 18

Coll: Friedrich Sarre, Ascona
Lit: 1902   Bode p. 88, Pl. 52
          1941   Erdmann pp. 175 178 Ill. 19 (Kirman)
          1960   Erdmann p. 40 Ill. 74 (Kirman c. 1600)
          1968   Ellis p. 19 (Kirman mid-16th century)

34

The wealth of large floral motifs conceals the fact that this is a three-plane lattice design, one system made up of ivory leaflets, the other two of red and of blue bract-stems respectively. This carpet, formerly in the possession of Professor Friedrich Sarre, Director of the Berlin Museums, is today regarded in the museum as late sixteenth century. It is one of the most elegant of the type. All the details are beautifully drawn and primary motifs include, besides the usual handsome palmettes and rosettes, vases without brackets and sickle leaves overlying palmettes. The fact that primary devices, even when diagonally placed, retain their shape

35

Three-plane lattice design with a background of floral scrolls on a deep blue field.

Woollen-pile carpet fragment, Shāh ʿAbbās period.
Width: 71 cm (2 ft 4 in)
Length: 122 cm (4 ft)

Victoria and Albert Museum, London, Inv. 242–1896.

The design of this fragment, to which little attention has been paid, is a mirror image of the lower left corner of the field of the Berlin fragment (no. 34), but a strip of field which would unite the two is missing. The colours used in corresponding motifs sometimes differ, which is not unusual in such rugs.

A fragment similar in design but smaller than no. 34, with a run of border from the right side of the rug, was also at one time in the Sarre Collection. It is known only from a poor photograph but it could be continuous in length with this piece from the Victoria and Albert Museum. A vase and adjoin-

ing motifs correspond to those at the top of the Berlin fragment (no. 34). No measurements of the smaller Sarre piece from the right side of a carpet are known but, by the design, it and the exhibited fragment must equal in length the Berlin piece from the left side of the rug.

It would seem that all the fragments are from one carpet.

36

Three-plane lattice design with a background of floral scrolls on a red field.

Woollen-pile carpet fragment, 17th century.
Width: 119 cm (3 ft 10½ in)
Length: 218 cm (7 ft 1½ in)

Burrell Collection, Glasgow Art Gallery and Museum, Inv. 9–10.

This design exemplifies a later stage of the three-plane lattice design in nos. 33–35. It is so rich in motifs that

35

not only are the floral scrolls as well as the stems difficult to trace, but the whole design has become overcrowded and less well defined. There is also a certain angularity and lack of precision in the drawing of some of the large leaves and other motifs.

Another long field fragment[1] of this richly decorated style is in the Türk ve Islam Eserleri Museum in Istanbul.

Acq. from: Elie Afoumado, Nantwich, 1925

[1] Inv. 656

37

Three-plane lattice design with a background of floral scrolls on a red field. The S-stems terminating in graceful floral sprays bear palmettes and rosettes on the deep blue border.

Woollen-pile carpet fragment, Shāh 'Abbās period.
Width: 146 cm (4 ft 9½ in)
Length: 110 cm (3 ft 7 in)

Burrell Collection, Glasgow Art Gallery and Museum, Inv. 9.21.

This sadly worn and pieced fragment must once have been part of a splendid carpet. It shows clearly the erosion of red yarn which sometimes occurs in 'Vase'-technique rugs. This phenomenon, due apparently to the chemical reactions involved in the dyeing, which results in brittle fibres, is much more commonly seen in yarn dyed with dark brown or black.

The border exemplifies yet again an early stage of what ultimately became the stiff little floral squares – the 'frozen' border of late rugs – made up of rows of tiny blossoms and fruit.

Acq. from: A. Balian & Son, 1936
Lit: 1961 Beattie p. 6
Exh: 1936 Perth Museum (54)

38

Border of a shaped carpet with alternately reversed S-stems terminating in sprays of flowers with a rosette or palmette on the diagonals of the stems, and palmettes on their points of contact. Floral S-stems on the deep blue outer guard; and a reciprocal yellow and brown inner guard.

Woollen-pile carpet fragment, 17th century.
Width: 274 cm (9 ft)
Length 180.4 cm (5 ft 11 in)

Victoria and Albert Museum, London, Inv. 994–1886.

37

38

Although the border design closely resembles that of the previous fragment the effect is slightly distorted. The rosettes, separated by palmettes, are not quite symmetrical in both directions, as a rosette should be, nor are the palmettes balanced bilaterally. This slight distortion of the design comes from the shaping of the carpet. It is exhibited with the warps vertical as they would be when extended between the beams of the loom. From this and the change of direction of the outer guard next to the yellow vine leaf palmette, it is evident that the carpet was of unusual shape. The relative gracefulness of the border design should be compared with nos. 33, 34 and 37.

Lit: 1968   Beattie p. 4 (Kirman 17th century)

39

Border design of red, orange and ivory interlaced arabesques on a background of floral scrolls.

Woollen-pile carpet fragments, 17th century.
Width: 142 cm (4 ft 8 in)
Length: 174 cm (5 ft 8½ in)

Burrell Collection, Glasgow Art Gallery and Museum, Inv. 9.14.

This design is so striking that other fragments in various museums are immediately recognizable. The shades of colour in the arabesques vary somewhat from one part of the rug to another, and so too do the number of tiny decorative motifs on the scrolling stems of the border background. These appear to be more numerous at the beginning of the rug, as if later the weavers had wearied of introducing such small embellishments.

The fragments from the lower left corner should be compared with that from the upper right (no. 36). The upper left corner, which may be the piece illustrated by Martin[1] was in the Acheroff Collection and is now in the Louvre.[2] Another fragment,[3] also in the Louvre, is from the same end of the rug and is virtually a mirror image of the lower border adjoining the corner of the fragments exhibited here (see no. 40).

Acq. from: Agop Balian, 1934

[1] Fig. 179
[2] MAO–491 B–1
[3] MAO–491 B–2

40

Three-plane lattice design with a background of floral scrolls on a red field. Three interlaced systems of broad red, orange and ivory arabesques and fine floral scrolls decorate the deep blue border, between yellow and ivory S-stem guards.

Woollen-pile carpet fragment, 17th century.
Width: 95 cm (3 ft 1½ in)
Length: 206 cm (6 ft 9 in)

Museum of Fine Arts, Boston, Inv. 64–2102.

Carpet fragments of this handsome and well-known design, scattered about in various museums, are so numerous that one wonders whether they are from one or more than one carpet. The best preserved pieces are in the Musée des Tissus[1] in Lyons and in the Victoria and Albert Museum[2] in London. The design is monumental befitting a large carpet and the general style of the field design is that of the somewhat later, purple-ground piece in Lyons (see no. 41). In both these carpets the smaller size of the intermediate motifs in relation to the large primary forms reduces crowding in the field and emphasizes the primary motifs.

This fragment is from the upper right corner of the carpet and the border corner is a mirror image of the upper left in the Louvre. The design in these two fragments differs from that of the lower left corner (no. 39) in Glasgow. It does not necessarily follow that they are from different carpets because corner designs at one end of a rug may differ from those at the other end. This peculiarity is more common in Indian and Indo-Persian than in Persian carpets.

To judge from the field design and from the gradual diminution in the number of little decorative elements on the background scrolls of various border

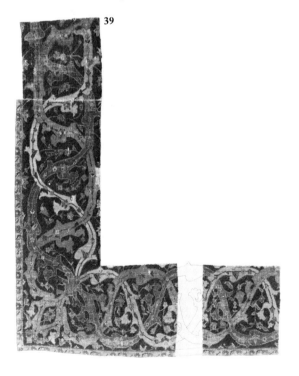

39

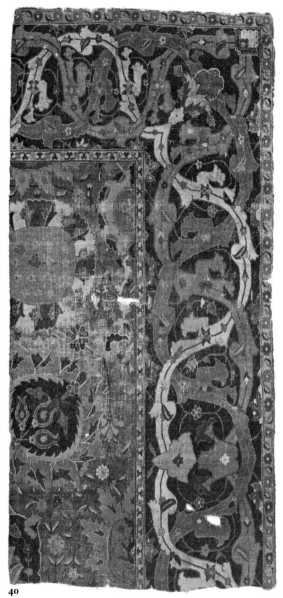

40

fragments, pieces from the right side of the carpet (with a few sections, including the lower right corner, missing) could begin with the Paris fragment[3] and be followed by the London, Lyons and Boston pieces.

Much of the field of the rug and of the left border are missing, but besides the end fragments and the left corners mentioned above, other parts of a left border are in the Louvre,[4] the Museum of Decorative Art[5] in Copenhagen and in the Hermitage,[6] the latter still with some field attached. Comparative measurements have not been made but the impression gained from a study of the fragments is that they may all be from one carpet, and certain other field

fragments without border may eventually prove to
be from the same piece.

Broad arabesques in a more simplified form,
aligned along the field like parallel borders, characterized a large Indo-Persian rug once in the Jaipur
Collection, and field designs of strap-like arabesques
were discussed by Erdmann[7] in relation to the famous
carpet in Hamburg.

[1] Inv. 28–153 Migeon 1903b Pl. 82
[2] Inv. 453–1884; Surv. Pl. 1220
[3] Arts Decs. Inv. 10556
[4] Inv. MAO–49–B–3
[5] 74.1920A
[6] Inv. V.T. 997
[7] 1961 p. 150

Coll: M. Ispénian, Cairo
  Mrs Edward Jackson Holmes
Lit: 1932 Wiet p. 199 Pl. XLIV (Isfahan 17th
     century)
   1933 Wiet p. 89 Pl. XLVII (17th century)
Exh: 1931 London (276) (17th century)

41

Three-plane lattice design on a dark purple field, with
a background of floral scrolls.

Woollen-pile carpet fragment, 17th–18th century.
Width: 240 cm (7 ft 10½ in)
Length: 59 cm (1 ft 11 in)

Musée des Tissus, Lyons, Inv. 25–385.

The use of purple as a field colour is rare but not
unique and as a considerable space of time separates
no. 25 and this fragment it can hardly have been just
a temporary fashion.

The strip is part of the field of a larger fragment
(included in the illustration) which belongs to the
same museum. The design is a more stylized version
of no. 40. From comparison with the much earlier
examples of a three-plane lattice design (nos. 33–35)
it is apparent that the motifs now lack detail, are much
squarer in form and are aligned more rigidly, and the
broad arabesques in the border are reduced to their
simplest form, all of which one would expect in a late
descendant of a more splendid design.

Similar field and border designs appear in rugs
from other weaving districts, as comparison with no.
42 shows.

A large fragment[1] of somewhat earlier date on a
dark blue field, similar to this in field, border and
guard designs is in the Textile Museum, Washington.

[1] Ellis 1968 Fig. 6

Lit: 1968 Ellis p. 18 note 24

42

Three-plane lattice design with a background of
floral scrolls on a red field. Pairs of broad arabesques,
the red directed outwards, the blue inwards, decorate
the blue border, between deep blue and orange and
blue guards.

Woollen-pile carpet fragments, probably 18th cen-
tury.
Width: 289.5 cm (9 ft 6 in)
Length: 88 cm (2 ft 10½ in)

Metropolitan Museum of Art, New York, Inv.
22.100.69.

Originally this carpet must have been much longer,
but in its present form the warps are shorter than the
wefts. When published in 1923 Breck and Morris
realized there was something odd about it, but overlooked the fact that the border adjoining the large
ivory palmette, which differs slightly from the other
three, was woven opposite in direction to the rest of
the rug.

The primary motifs are squared off and arranged
in conspicuous vertical lines much as in no. 41. Both
pieces have the strap-like arabesque borders which

41

are used with three-plane large-leaf lattice designs, and are frequently associated with bicoloured reciprocal guards.

Although the design is similar to those of pieces just discussed, this rug comes from another area. It is woven in the symmetrical or Turkish knot and its limited colour range should be compared with the wide range of lovely colours used in typical 'Vase'-technique rugs. A single-plane lattice design with flowering plants in the spaces, the same border design as this and a restricted colour scheme is in the Musée des Arts Décoratifs in Paris.[1] It also may be Kurdish.

During the eighteenth century there seems to have been a marked movement of this and other designs, notably to the Bijar district and the Caucasus, an occurrence usually explained by civil disruption, which may have caused the migration of weavers to other centres. It is possible of course that the inspiration of great and colourful designs was in itself enough to explain copying elsewhere.

[1] Inv. 10548
Coll: James F. Ballard

Exh: 1923 New York (9) (late 17th or early 18th century)

43

Three-plane lattice design on a rust field. The deep blue border contains stylized sprays of flowers between a red guard with yellow cartouches and a blue-green guard with S-stems.

Woollen-pile carpet fragment, probably late 17th century.
Width: 45.5 cm (1 ft 6 in)
Length: 88.5 cm (2 ft 11 in)

Baltimore Museum of Art (gift of Mr and Mrs J. R. Herbert Boone), Inv. 59.40.

A large worn fragment of a rust-ground, three-plane lattice rug[1] in the Textile Museum in Washington has a border in the same colour and design as this fragment. The little yellow cartouches in the outer guard appear in both, and the two pieces may be parts of the same carpet. If this be so it is the only example known to me of a three-plane lattice rug in this colour.

[1] Ellis 1968 Fig. 4

42

44 (not illustrated)

Three-plane lattice design with a background of floral scrolls.

Woollen-pile carpet fragments, 17th century.
a)
Width: 54 cm (1 ft 9 in)
Length: 139 cm (4 ft 3 in)
b)
Width: 60 cm (1 ft 11½ in)
Length: 113 cm (3 ft 8½ in)

Iraq Museum, Baghdad.

Erdmann once pointed out that the only known example of a green-ground Vase carpet was in Baghdad and this exhibit is to show the colour. Two long fragments with broad yellow and blue arabesques on an orange border were in the Mirjan Sarai in 1962 but only recently has it become known that photographs exist of at least seven fragments apparently of one large carpet. The field design is a typical three-plane lattice surrounded by a late arabesque border.

Lit: 1968 Ellis p. 18

45

Three-plane lattice design with a background of floral scrolls on a rich yellow field. Pairs of broad arabesques on a blue border rise from a palmette and meet adjoining arabesques, the green directed outwards, the red inwards. Red and chestnut reciprocal guard.

Woollen-pile carpet fragment, 17th century.
Width: 63 cm (2 ft 1 in)
Length: 90 cm (2 ft 11 in)

Burrell Collection, Glasgow Art Gallery and Museum, Inv. 9–17.

It is uncommon to find a three-plane lattice design on a yellow field. Furthermore the arabesque border differs from the more familiar type such as that of no. 13. It lacks the usual little stems terminating in leaflets which normally swing out from the tips of the palmettes (see nos. 13 and 32) and the palmette itself is more conspicuous due to an increase in size, the serration of the edges and the lateral protrusions which contrast in colour with the rest of the motif.

In 1973 the Iparmüvészeti Museum in Budapest acquired a large fragment[1] in the same design and also with a yellow field. It is reduced in length, and has a border attached in the manner of no. 42. The border is similar to the Burrell piece but more angular and the two pieces are not therefore from one carpet. It may be that this type of arabesque border is characteristic of the work of a specific group of weavers.

Acq. from: A. Maurice & Co. 1934

[1] Inv. 73–186

43

45

46

Three-plane lattice design with a background of floral scrolls on an ivory field. On the red border, pairs of arabesques rise from the base of serrated palmettes, the blue directed outwards, the yellow inwards. A mid-blue inner guard remains with orange cartouches and dark green lobed lozenges; narrow stepped subguard.

Woollen-pile carpet, 19th century(?).
Width: 64 cm (2 ft 1½ in)
Length: 175 cm (5 ft 9½ in)

Textile Museum, Washington, D.C., Inv. R 33.6.1.

There are a number of unusual features in this design – the ivory field with the background scrolls breaking into sprays of flowers, the wide spacing between the large primary motifs, the dragon's head terminating the handle of a vase, and the wide inner guard. With the exception of the dragon's head these are all found in what is probably the world's most published Vase

carpet – the white-ground fragment[1] in the Museum für Angewande Kunst in Vienna. It has generally been supposed that the Washington fragment is another part of the Vienna, or at least a similar, antique carpet. In recent years however, because of a certain fuzziness on the under surface, the suspicion has been aroused that the Washington piece may be late Tabriz work.[2] Such a suggestion having been made it cannot be lightly dismissed and it inevitably again raises the question as to whether the exhibited fragment is a copy, or a part, of the Vienna rug. Technically, according to notes, they seem to be alike even to the five-ply warps, but when I examined the Vienna fragment in 1974 I was not convinced that they were exactly the same. The same conclusion was reached independently by Mr Charles Grant Ellis in 1975. The difficulty of assessing the finer points of two pieces at such a distance is obvious. The small sickle leaf on one of the stems of the exhibited fragment and some of the border details are more angular than similar details in the Vienna carpet and the cartouches in the guard of the latter are slimmer than in the Washington fragment. One of our great regrets is that the Vienna rug is not available for the exhibition and the problem of the relationship of the two pieces may now remain unresolved for years.

Quite apart from the actual date of weaving of the exhibited fragment, the period to which the design has been assigned needs reassessing. The borders of the white-ground pieces are more stylized versions of those in the yellow-ground fragment (no. 45), the more angularly designed piece in Budapest, and the arabesque and palmette rug illustrated by Martin.[3] In addition the wide spacing between the primary field motifs, as well as the multiplicity of little flowers, all point to a late date. Even the width of the inner guard proportionate to that of the main stripe, in the Vienna carpet, is unusual. Whatever the date of weaving of the Washington fragment, the design would seem more appropriate to the eighteenth than to the seventeenth century.

Most authors simply give 'Persia' as the provenance of the Vienna rug. More specific attributions are: 'Probably South Persian',[4] Joshagan,[5] Kirman.[6] Dating is sixteenth or second half of the sixteenth century, but Kendrick and Tattersall[7] suggest seventeenth century.

[1] Surv. Pl. 1224; Inv. O.359
[2] Ellis 1968 note 51
[3] Pl. XIX
[4] Troll Pl. 14
[5] Surv. Pl. 1224
[6] Heinz 1956 No. 19
[7] 1922 p. 24 Pl. 18

Lit: 1940   Ettinghausen p. 110 Fig. 4 (c.1600)
        1968   Ellis Fig. 7 note 51
Exh: 1940   New York Gal. I No. 1 (c.1600)

46

47

Three-plane lattice design with a background of flowering plants on a blue field. Units of a palmette (clasped by arabesques), from which spring stems terminating in elaborate 'irises', alternate with rosettes on a yellow background, between blue and reciprocal blue and yellow guards.

47

Woollen-pile carpet fragment, second quarter 17th century.
Width: 178 cm (5 ft 10 in)
Length: 363 cm (11 ft 11 in)

Fogg Art Museum, Harvard University, Cambridge, Mass. (gift of Joseph V. McMullan), Inv. 1962–346.

This is one of the loveliest of the so-called Vase carpets and the serenity of the design is the antithesis of the dynamic style of nos. 33–36. The background of flowering plants, here including a windswept willow, unlike the more numerous examples with floral scrolls, imparts direction to the design which begins with the horizontally placed half-palmettes already mentioned (p. 27). An alternative to a floral or vase-on-bracket motif is that made up of stripes in chevron style, such as appear in some guards. Occasionally vases are similarly decorated. Originally the field was probably one-third as wide again since the usual three-plane lattice design has two whole ogives in the width.

Similar borders occur in the beautiful William Morris fragment in the Victoria and Albert Museum[1] and in a Flowering-plant rug formerly in the Mc-Mullan Collection,[2] both of which have red fields.

The renewal of the side and end borders was done at a period when western dyes were not stable and the colours which originally must have matched the rest of the carpet are worth studying because they show a degree of fading which can occur within a century. Some of the other three-plane lattice designs in which flowering plants are used in the lattice spaces instead of the more usual floral scrolls are to be found in Amsterdam,[3] Baltimore,[4] Boston,[5] Chicago,[6] London,[7,8] Lyons,[9] Paris.[10] The whereabouts of the Ginzkey carpet[11] and one illustrated by Martin[12] are unknown. The borders of the Chicago and Lyons rugs are filled with directionally arranged flowering plants, one immediately above the other in the manner of certain Mughal Flowering-plant carpets.

[1] Inv. 719–1897; Surv. Pl. 1227
[2] Islamic Carpets 17
[3] Ryks 518
[4] M. of Art 59.39
[5] MFA. 08.438 and fragments
[6] Art Inst. No. unknown
[7] Priv. poss. formerly Brown, Surv. Pl. 1228
[8] V&A 164–1897 719–1897
[9] Lyons 25.586
[10] Louvre MAO–491–C
[11] Bode/Kühnel 1922 Ill. 36
[12] Fig. 182

Coll: Heinrich Jacoby
       B. Altmann & Co.
       Joseph V. McMullan

Lit: 1923 Jacoby Pl. 2 (Persia 17th century)
       1923 Altmann & Co. Pl. II (Persia 17th century)
       1965 McMullan 16 (Persian, School of Shāh ʿAbbās)
Exh: 1926 Chicago (20) (Joshagan first third 17th century)
       1949 Cambridge, Mass. (3)
       1966 Washington (10) (Persian 17th century)
       1970 New York (72) (Kirman end 16th century)
       1972 London (16)

48

Palmette and stem design based on a three-plane lattice pattern with flowering plants on a mid-blue field. The pink border has pairs of arabesques, the blue directed outwards, the pink inwards, between guards of equal width.

Woollen-pile carpet, 19th–20th century.
Width: 156 cm (5 ft 1½ in)
Length: 249 cm (8 ft 2 in)

John Hewett.

48

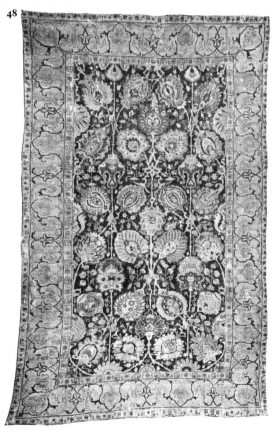

This is an excellent example of the failure of a forgery. The drawing of the motifs with their curious details and the arrangement of the stems should be compared with those of the three-plane lattice designs in antique carpets in which vertical stems do not extend throughout the length of the rug. The plan of the border is similar to no. 30, but little coiled motifs are used instead of background scrolls. An ornate silk-pile, shaped rug[1] in the Textile Museum is also of late date and has an equally misunderstood design.

The antiquing process has involved patching of the field with pieces from the upper end of the rug, which is reduced in length, and abrading the surface to give the impression of wear. The original cochineal shade of red has faded and there has been some painting over of colours. All this would not deceive anyone familiar with antique rugs, but it might deceive someone unfamiliar with them, and it shows the lengths to which the unscrupulous will go to create 'antiques'.

Pieces with much more accurate designs exist which are not easy to assess. It is difficult to say if some, referred to as eighteenth century, are, in fact, of that date or are well-done reproductions, now showing a little wear, which, although originally not intended to deceive, are now being passed off as much earlier rugs.

[1] Ellis 1968 Fig. 17

49 (Colour Plate 10)

Three-plane large-leaf lattice design with lattice spaces in contrasting colours, each containing four large motifs and their accompanying floral scrolls. Remains of a reciprocal guard.

Woollen-pile carpet fragments, 17th century.
Width: 178 cm (5 ft 10½ in)
Length: 353 cm (11 ft 8½ in)

Textile Museum, Washington, D.C., Inv. R 33.6.3.

The most striking feature of the design is the lattice of large serrated leaves decorated in a variety of ways and at times even formed of pairs of leaves of different colours one apparently growing out of the other. The vase-and-bracket motif, as well as large rosettes and palmettes, also characterize this type of design, and the richness and variety of field colours, instead of the customary single colour, approximate to a magnificent sampler. Here the lattice spaces contain only four, instead of the usual six, motifs found in the rugs with monochrome fields, but there is also a six-motif group with multicoloured fields. Border designs are either of broad arabesques or 'frozen' floral sprays.

A considerable number of pieces exist, but no undamaged carpet of the type is known, although the example in Istanbul shows the full length.[1]

Examples with six large motifs in the spaces are in London,[2] Paris,[3] Philadelphia,[4] and Sarajevo,[5] and with four in Amsterdam,[6] Berlin,[7] Detroit,[8] Istanbul,[9] Leningrad,[10] London,[11] Munich,[12] Paris,[13] Sarajevo,[14] Washington,[15] and formerly in the Baranovicz Collection. Tiny fragments are in the Museum für Kunsthandwerk in Frankfurt, in the Boston Museum of Fine Arts and at Firma Bernheimer in Munich; and D'Allemagne illustrates a small fragment.[16]

The exhibited pieces have a heavy backshag and so too do quite a number of those just mentioned, some of which must be from the same carpets.

Erdmann in 1941 regarded the Berlin fragment[17] as early sixteenth century, the Sarajevo piece[18] from the end of that century or the beginning of the seventeenth, and the Cassirer carpet[19] as sixteenth century; and he suggested an origin in 'Kirman (?)'. The usual dating given to such pieces is sixteenth–seventeenth century, but in view of the border designs a date in the mid-seventeenth century or even later would seem more appropriate in most instances.

Designs somewhat similar to this large-leaf lattice type, if they also included animals, were no doubt the prototypes for the Dragon carpets of the Caucasus.

[1] Martin Fig. 186
[2] V&A 220–1892
[3] Arts Dec. 27656
[4] P.M.A. 55.65.8
[5] Ethn. Mus. 1047
[6] Rijks. 12016
[7] Staat. Mus. 89136
[8] Art Inst. Cassirer Coll.
[9] T.ve.I. T1004
[10] Hermitage 7508
[11] V&A 1067–1901
[12] Völkerkunde 14.47.34
[13] Louvre MAO–491–A
[14] Ethn. Mus. 1002
[15] Text. Mus. R33.6.2
[16] Opp. p. 98
[17] Ill. 21
[18] Ill. 22
[19] Ill. 20

Lit: 1939   Surv. p. 2453 note 4
       1968   Ellis p. 25 Fig. 9 (Kirman)
Exh: 1931   London
       1967   Washington

49

50

Two-plane leaflet-lattice design in which the leaflet-stems enclose areas of contrasting colours. In the centre of each a large floral motif, with its accompanying scrolling vine, covers the conjunctions of the secondary lattice stems. Rosettes, palmettes and sprays of little flowers decorate the deep blue-green border.

Woollen-pile carpet fragments, Shāh 'Abbās period.
Width: 96.5 cm (3 ft 2½ in)
Length: 360 cm (11 ft 11 in)

Textile Museum, Washington, D.C., Inv. R 33.6.4

In spite of their condition, these fragments exhibit the beautiful colour, the graceful curves and the attractive border of what is the earliest known example of this design. Even each leaflet of the primary lattice has a well-defined little scroll at the base.

In an equally pieced, but late, example[1] in the Burrell Collection the leaflet-stems outlining the different colours of the field are so stylized that they resemble chains of fish hooks, and the background vines become a network of stiff stems.

The Textile Museum rug is of special importance in showing that others of this type (cf no. 51) are in the tradition of a once splendid design which persisted over a long period, and, certainly in the seventeenth century, are not just variants of another design.

[1] Inv. 9–16

Lit: 1968 Ellis p. 25 Fig. 8 (Kirman 16th century)

51

Two-plane leaflet-lattice carpet in which leaflet stems enclose areas of contrasting colours, each containing a large single motif on the secondary lattice-system or a filling of numerous small blossoms. Rosettes, palmettes, 'irises' and squares of little flowers with connecting stems are arranged on a red border between narrow guards.

Woollen-pile carpet, second half 17th century.
Width: 269 cm (8 ft 10 in)
Length: 706 cm (23 ft 2 in)

Baltimore Museum of Art (gift of Sadie A. May), Inv. 42–59.

Among the large single motifs contained in the lattice spaces are palmettes, rosettes and other devices familiar in three-plane lattice designs. The fine stems of the secondary lattice which unite the single motifs have lost the graceful curves seen in no. 50 but, as in that carpet, they change colour as they pass from one lattice to another.

This carpet is a pair to the famous Berlin piece[1] destroyed during the last war, and the many observations concerning that design are equally applicable to the Baltimore rug. The colours in one are a mirror image of those in the other, which would create a pleasant bilateral colour symmetry if the two carpets, as has been suggested, were originally intended to lie side by side.

Pope[2] regarded the three-plane large-leaf lattice design (cf. no. 49) of the well-known carpet in Istanbul,[3] which has the same type of border as this, as a 'further conventionalization of the type', referring presumably to rugs in this two-plane leaflet-lattice style. This and the Istanbul carpet might be regarded as contemporary, but one would hardly regard the exhibited carpet as being much earlier than the other, and the evidence of the Washington fragment (no. 50) proves the design to be one of long standing.

Originally the Berlin rug was regarded as sixteenth[4] or early seventeenth century[5] but Ellis's[6] reassessment of the chronology seems reasonable. He points to the stiffening, already mentioned, of graceful sprays of flowers which eventually assume the

50

form of little squares – the so-called 'frozen' border seen here. That, the angularity of the secondary lattice stems, and the filling of entire spaces with multiple blossoms, which occurs in rugs with late borders, point to a date probably not earlier than the mid-seventeenth century. Besides the Berlin rug and the Burrell carpet mentioned in no. 50, other pieces were in the Miss Brown Collection in Glasgow[7] and in Cairo.[8] Pope of course considered the provenance Joshagan,[9] and Erdmann[10] Kirman and sixteenth century.

[1] Surv. Pl. 1222
[2] Surv. p. 2380
[3] Bode/Kühnel 1958 No. 95
[4] von Scala IX
[5] Surv. Pl. 1222
[6] 1968 p. 19
[7] Surv. Pl. 1221
[8] Wiet 1935 Pl. 18
[9] Surv. Pl. 1222
[10] 1960 No. 70

Coll: French & Co.
       Clarence H. Mackay
       Sadie A. May
Lit: 1935 Dimand Fig. 5 (Vase rug, Persian, end 16th century)
       1955 Anon p. 88
       1968 Ellis p. 25
       1973 Dimand/Mailey p. 72 Fig. 103 (end 16th century)
Exh: 1935 New York
       1937 San Francisco (Persian 16th century)
       1947 Chicago (6) (late 16th or early 17th century)

52

Two-plane lattice design with multiple simulated medallions of lozenge shape in various colours on a deep red field. A dark blue border with S-stems terminating in serrated leaves and bearing palmettes and rosettes lies between a pink and blue-green reciprocal outer, and an ivory inner guard.

Woollen-pile carpet, date uncertain.
Width: 287 cm (9 ft 5 in)
Length: 749 cm (24 ft 7 in)

Victoria and Albert Museum, London, Inv. 127–1884.

Unlike the designs with contrasting colours enclosed in leaflet-stems (nos. 50 and 51) there is no change in field colour in this two-plane lattice design. Only a few bracts or rosettes decorate the stems and both systems bear the familiar rather large palmettes, rosettes, irises and vases. Lobed and pointed lozenges surround the vertical motifs on the conjunctions of one stem-system only. These units then dominate

the design and are made more conspicuous by enclosing colours contrasting with that of the field. They are not true medallions but rather similar enclosures of different colour through which the stems pass to continue their course along the field. Offset rows of large medallion-like ogives are used in the Multiple-medallion Sarajevo carpet of 1656 and Pope (*Survey*) grouped the London carpet with it.

Unusual grey cotton second wefts were noted in both the London and the Sarajevo carpet, which was woven for the shrine at Mahan, and 'drab' was recorded for the second wefts of no. 9 which has the same border design. Whether or not the yarn is actually alike and a technical peculiarity of one group can only be judged with rugs side by side.

The London carpet was bought in the Bon Marché in Paris in 1884 and its condition is so excellent that it has raised the question as to the possibility of its being an eighteenth-century piece. Because of its somewhat unusual design it never quite fitted in with any past groupings of Vase carpets, but when compared with the Williamsburg carpet (no. 53) in particular, and the two-plane leaflet-lattice designs just discussed, it is evident that they form a fairly closely related group.

Lit: 1908   Martin Fig. 189 (Kirman c.1650)
      1908   Scala, Bode, Sarre Pl. XXIV (Persian c.1600)
      1920   Kendrick p. 17 Pl. VI and 1931 p. 14 Pl. VI (Persian 16th or 17th century)
      1922   Kendrick & Tattersall p. 24 Pl. 19 (Persian 17th century)
      1923   Pope p. 327 (probably Kirman last quarter 16th century)
      1939   Surv. p. 2381 Pl. 1237 (Joshagan mid-17th century)
      1958   Bode/Kühnel p. 136
      1962   Ellis p. 40 Fig. 13
      1963   Schlosser No. 56 (Northwest Persia c.1600)

53

Two-plane lattice design with multiple simulated medallions of cartouche and lozenge shape in various colours on a deep red field. Dark blue border with S-stems terminating in flower sprays, palmettes and rosettes.

Woollen-pile carpet, late 17th century (?).
Width: 155 cm (5 ft 1 in)
Length: 325 cm (10 ft 8 in)

Colonial Williamsburg Foundation, Williamsburg, Virginia, Inv. 1963–729.

The colouring of this rug is attractive and although reduced in length it is well preserved.

Basically it is a two-plane lattice design but the effect is crowded and it is difficult to trace the stem-systems. There are several reasons for this. The practice of changing the colour of the stems, especially as they enter the simulated medallions (see nos. 50 and 51), continues here, although the field of the carpet like that of no. 52 is monochrome. The customary fine stems of the scrolling vines are given much the same value as those of the lattice stems which are normally more conspicuous, and the placing of a simulated medallion on the conjunctions of the stems of both lattices instead of just on one as in no. 52 all combine to obscure the clarity of the design, and point to its misunderstanding and to a late date.

Lit: 1975 Lanier No. 16 (Kirman 17th century)

53

54

Single-plane lattice design of arabesques and plants directionally arranged on an ochre field. Alternately reversed pairs of green and dark blue arabesques on the red border are separated by angularly lobed lozenges and linked by subsidiary floral scrolls. Guards are yellow and dark blue.

Woollen-pile carpet fragment, 17th century.
Width: 115.5 cm (3 ft 9½ in)
Length: 124 cm (4 ft 1 in)

Musée du Louvre, Paris, Inv. MAO–491–D.

This is one of the fragments that Martin illustrated in 1908. The type of arabesque used to form the lattice in this design differs from those commonly found in Arabesque carpets and the motif on the conjunctions of the stems is considerably larger than that used in known single-plane lattice designs. Another unusual feature is that the pairs of border arabesques, the tips of which overlap each other, have no true connection with the lozenges. This arrangement occurs in the border of the 'Vase'-technique rug no. 58. Judging by the design, a fragment from the Baranovicz Collection is about the same length, and originally may have been attached to the side of this piece. It may be the second of the fragments, mentioned by Erdmann, which were once in the possession of Sarre.

Lit: 1908 Martin Fig. 195 (Kirman c.1600)
1941 Erdmann p. 184 note 214

54

55 (Colour Plate 11)

Single-plane lattice design enclosing flowering plants, on an ivory field. The border is red with pairs of slim arabesques alternately reversed on a floral scroll background, between deep blue guards.

Woollen-pile carpet fragment, 17th century.
Width: 76 cm (2 ft 6 in)
Length: 94 cm (3 ft 1 in)

Kunstmuseum, Düsseldorf, Inv. 11047.

Simple attractive designs are found in Single-plane Lattice carpets. A small fragment with a soft blue field, and vine leaves similar to those on the conjunctions of the stems, illustrated in this fragment, is in the Hermitage Museum,[1] and a fragment on darker blue with a yellow lattice, in the Erlenmeyer Collection in 1970, has, in addition to the flowering plants, a motif of stiff little flowering trees enclosing a cypress.

[1] Inv. V.T. 1062

Lit: 1941 Erdmann p. 184
      1942 Erdmann p. 410
      1968 Ellis p. 26
Exh: 1950 Hamburg (80) (Kirman 17th century)
      1971 Hamburg and Frankfurt (21) (Kirman 17th century)

55

56

Single-plane lattice design with flowering plants directionally arranged on a yellow field. Cypresses and flowering plants alternate on a red border, between ivory and multicoloured guards.

Woollen-pile carpet fragments, 18th century.
Width: 141.5 cm (4 ft 8 in)
Length: 162 cm (5 ft 4 in)

Textile Museum, Washington, D.C., Inv. R 33.3.1.

The blue bract-stems of this single-plane lattice design bear little inverted trefoil leaves on the junctions of the stems, which to some extent counteract the directional effect of the flowering plants. The border is a late version of one row of field motifs as used in no. 14 and shows how a section of field design may be used for a border.

Lit: 1968 Ellis p. 26 Fig. 11 (Kirman 18th century)

57

Single-plane lattice-leaf design on a deep blue field. The long serrated leaves, overlying stems, enclose lattice spaces filled with flowering plants or shrubs which occasionally rise from small vases on brackets.

Woollen-pile carpet, 18th century or later (?).
Width: 101.5 cm (3 ft 4 in)
Length: 399 cm (13 ft 1 in)

Burrell Collection, Glasgow Art Gallery and Museum, Inv. 9–7.

Martin[1] collected fragments in this design from what he believed to be one large carpet, which he dated to about 1500. It had a wide arabesque border and fairly broad guard stripes. In 1939 Pope[2] reproduced a 'similar' piece from the collection of the Comtesse de Béhague. Its border was the same as the inner guard illustrated by Martin and, difficult as it is to tell from a photograph, it appears to be skilfully made up from fragments perhaps of the same carpet as the pieces illustrated by Martin. The design, with numerous blossoms crowded into so many spaces, and the style of the irises have not been found elsewhere in lattice designs of seventeenth-century 'Vase'-technique rugs, and they suggest a late date.

The exhibited piece is in remarkably good condition, and when examined recently, although it has no border, the right side was found to be finished with a two-cord overcast selvage and the left with an overcasting on the outer two warps. The colours used for the overcasting were the same as those in the pile, and multicoloured yarn was not seen in the wefts. The only other examples known to me personally are two small worn and joined fragments in Paris[3] with blue and brown first and third wefts. It would have been of interest to compare them structurally with the Glasgow piece, but, as they are not available, the latter must meanwhile remain a problem.

There appears to be no difference in the designs of the other fragments known only from the illustrations mentioned above. Erdmann[4] grouped the Béhague rug with Vase carpets, which he regarded as from Kirman, disagreeing with Pope's attribution to Joshagan, and he dated it to the mid-seventeenth century. He regarded the design as a late stage in evolution.

[1] p. 78 Fig. 184
[2] Surv. p. 2380 Pl. 1233
[3] Arts Dec. Inv. 17589
[4] 1941 p. 184

Acq. from: O. T. Milla 1916

57

56

58

Single-plane lattice design on an ochre field, with lobed octagram medallions, from the side terminals of which swing scrolling stems terminating in curved orange or violet leaves. The wine-red border bears alternately reversed pairs of arabesques enclosing lozenge-medallions, between paired outer and inner guards.

Woollen-pile carpet, 17th–18th century.
Width: 190 cm (6 ft 3 in)
Length: 160 cm (5 ft 3 in)

Musée des Tissus, Lyons, Inv. 30.259.

This fragment, part of a carpet which originally must have been of large size, has a more complex design than those of the usual Single-plane Lattice carpets. The form of lattice is reminiscent of a type used in Mughal carpets. The diagonally opposed curved leaves terminating the stems which rise from the sides of the medallions recall the arrangement in sickle-leaf designs, but here the leaves are small and inconspicuous. The same stems bear small clouds. Border and colour are comparable to no. 54.

A rug with this same field design, somewhat more stylized but of unknown colour and structure, was formerly in the Dumbarton Oaks Collection.[1] It had a 'Ginzkey' border. Two red-ground pieces, known from illustrations, differing mainly in length, with an even later version of the design, are stated to be from Central Persia (eighteenth century)[2] and Joshagan (c.1700).[3] Both have the cypress and flowering-tree borders with the little blossoms in 'frozen' forms.

58

The border design of a third piece, a long fragment in the Victoria and Albert Museum,[4] is closely related to this piece from Lyons, but the design of the pale yellow field is only distantly related to it. Technically the two pieces are completely different.

Other large fragments almost certainly from this same carpet, of which this is the best preserved, are in East Berlin (regarded as Kirman and early seventeenth century by Erdmann[5]), Philadelphia,[6] (Persian, seventeenth century) and St Louis.[7] Smaller fragments without borders are in Baltimore,[8] Budapest[9] and London (private possession).

[1] Inv. No. 4
[2] Oettingen & Grote-Hasenbalg 11 Pl. 32
[3] Schürman 1966 No. 38
[4] Inv. 48–1922
[5] 1943 Ill. 3
[6] P.M.A. 55.65.41
[7] City Art Mus. 47–30
[8] Mus. of Art 59–41
[9] Iparművészeti Mus. 14.752

59

Kirman rug with a directional design of cypresses, birds and a vase from which rise flowering stems on an ivory background. Dragon and lion combats in the corners, on dark blue. Palmettes clasped by leaves alternate with rosettes on the pinkish-red main stripe of the border, between yellow and dark blue outer, and dark blue and orange inner, guards.

Woollen-pile rug, before 1895.
Width: 130.5 cm (4 ft 3½ in)
Length: 195 cm (6 ft 5 in)

Anonymous loan.

The under surface of this rug bears a label inscribed in ink: 'Kerman Carpet. Property of Ella Sykes. Bought at Kerman S.E. Persia. 1895.' Miss Ella Sykes, sister of Sir Percy Sykes, bequeathed the carpet to the present owner.

The design has features reminiscent of much earlier rugs. Cypresses bisected by the side borders occur in a group of Indian prayer rugs. Between the trees stands a vase on a flat dish, here represented by the red band lying across the vase. A vase supported by a bracket is a familiar motif, but in this instance its fusion with the bracket shows the nineteenth-century craftsman's misunderstanding of an earlier form. The animal combats also hark back to classical rugs, but the difference in drawing is striking. The purplish brown dye found in a considerable number of the exhibited rugs occurs also in the border of this example. Designs which diverge less from the prototype than this, and which are devoid of animals, were fairly widespread in Persia at the turn of the century and have been noted not only in Kirman rugs but also in those from the Shiraz and Ferraghan areas.

60

Arabesque palmette and rosette design on a dark blue field.

Woollen-pile carpet fragment, 18th century.
Width: 182 cm (5 ft 11¾ in)
Length: 212 cm (7 ft)

Museum of Fine Arts, Boston, Inv. 11–3058.

Although, as recorded in notes, the structure of this rug resembles the 'vase'-technique, when examined the 'handle' was different, and it is introduced for comparison.

Coll: D. G. Kelekian
Dr and Mrs John W. Elliot (gift 1975)

59

60

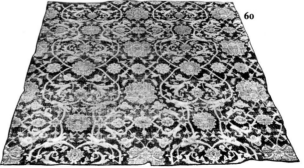

61

Fragment of border from an 'Ardabil' carpet with four pairs of opposed and joined arabesques on a background of floral scrolls, contained in an octafoil.

Woollen-pile carpet fragment, 946/1539–1540.
Width: 32.3 cm (13 in)
Length: 22.8 cm (9 in)

Burrell Collection, Glasgow Art Gallery and Museum, Inv. 9–120.

Two famous carpets, one in London and one in Los Angeles, long believed to have come from the shrine of the founder of the Safavid dynasty in Ardabil, both bear the signature 'Maqṣūd' of Kashan, and the date A.H. 946 (A.D. 1539/40). Although most authors seem to favour an origin in Tabriz there is no incontrovertible evidence to prove where these famous carpets were made, and in view of the signature, Kashan cannot entirely be ruled out. Dr Rexford Stead, who published a detailed study of the subject in 1974, points out that they may never even have been in the shrine at Ardabil.

The fragment is included in the exhibition to show the quality of the materials and the weave, which differ so greatly from those of the 'Vase'-technique rugs, and to give an idea of some of the colours, of these celebrated and much discussed carpets.

When the two carpets were restored, fragments apparently remained, mainly, like this, from the borders, but it is not known from which carpet the Burrell fragment came. These small pieces are now scattered about the world. The whereabouts of others are mentioned by Ellis[1] and Erdmann.[2] Another piece, somewhat larger than that exhibited, was, in 1969, in the Perez Collection in London. For the literature pertaining to the Ardabil carpets see Stead.

[1] 1964 p. 19
[2] 1970 p. 32

Acq. from: A. Balian   1954
Lit: 1961   Beattie p. 10
       1964   Ellis p. 19
       1970   Erdmann p. 32
Exh: 1967   Kendal (1)
       1969   Glasgow (47)

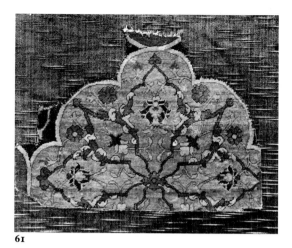

61

62

A cartouche and octafoil border design surrounded by scrolls and palmettes on a red background. Reciprocal-V subguards separate the main stripe from orange guards decorated with S-stems.

Woollen-pile carpet fragment, 16th century.
Width: 69 cm (2 ft 3 in)
Length: 155 cm (5 ft 1 in)

Keir Collection.

In 1926 Pope[1] pointed out the resemblance of the Stora Medallion carpet to the Ardabil, and suggested a possible provenance in Kashan, but in 1939 he grouped it with the Sanguszko carpets and considered it might be from Kirman,[2] a view with which Erdmann disagreed and again stressed its relationship to the Ardabil carpet. Unfortunately it is not available for the exhibition, but it was examined recently and the weave certainly differs from that of 'Vase'-technique rugs, not only in having all three wefts of dark wool, but because the second weft is so conspicuous. This border fragment when placed side by side with the Stora seemed of the same construction and is exhibited to give some idea of the weave of the Stora carpet. It is part of a larger fragment with a medallion and corner design on a deep blue field. The medallion is red, lobed and pointed and in this is not unlike that of the Stora, but it is edged with a broad ivory band. The colours in the cornerpiece are the reverse of those in the medallion.

Possibly the rugs in this weave may form a nucleus around which others can be grouped.

[1] Chicago No. 7
[2] Surv. Pl. 1211 p. 2350

Supplementary Plates

Eleven plates of rugs which it has not been possible to include in the exhibition, but which are used to supplement the text.

63. The Williams Medallion Carpet. Philadelphia Museum of Art (photograph by A. J. Wyatt, staff photographer).

64. The Cassirer Carpet, a medallion and corner design with animals and floral scrolls. Museum für Islamische Kunst, Stiftung Preussischer Kulturbesitz, Berlin, Federal Republic of Germany.

65. Medallion-and-corner design with animals, figures and floral scrolls, a so-called Sanguszko carpet. Victoria and Albert Museum, London.

66. A multiple-medallion design with a background of animals and floral scrolls, a so-called Sanguszko carpet. Musée des Tissus, Lyons.

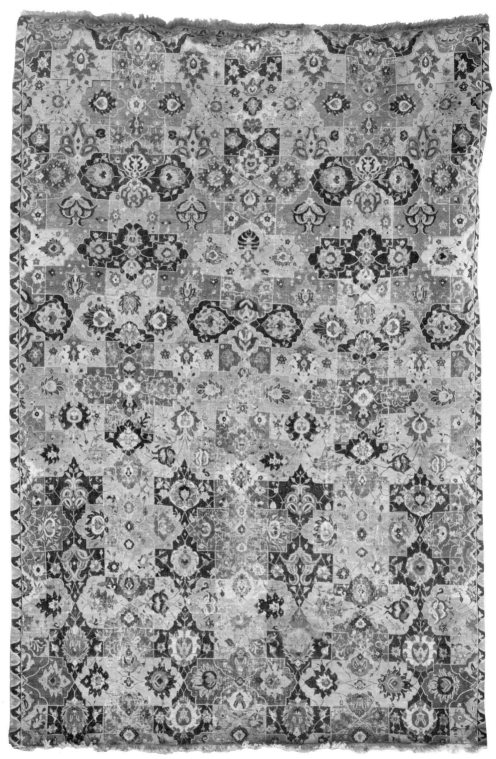

67. A multiple-medallion design of overlapping cartouches. The Metropolitan Museum of Art, New York (bequest of Horace Havemeyer, 1956).

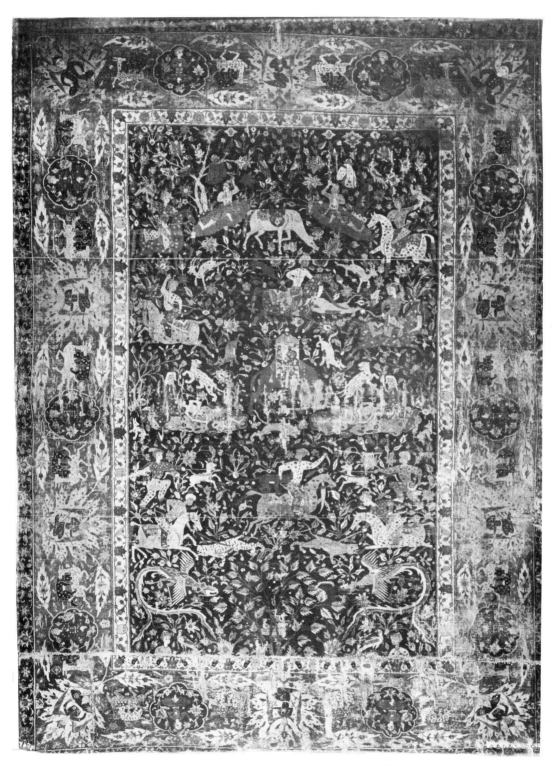

68. A directional design of little scenes, animals and trees. Musée des Arts Décoratifs, Paris.

69. A directional design of animals, figures and trees in the manner of a textile, a so-called Sanguszko carpet. Further destroyed during the last war. Staatliche Museen, zu Berlin, Islamisches Museum, Deutsche Demokratische Republik.

70. Sickle-leaf design. Fundação Calouste Gulbenkian, Lisbon.

71. Arabesque and animal design. The Metropolitan Museum of
Art, New York (gift of Mrs Harry Payne Bingham).

72. Single-plane lattice design of arabesques with flowering plants. Formerly Sarre Collection; present whereabouts unknown.

73. Shaped carpet fragment in a floral design. Ross Collection, Museum of Fine Arts, Boston.

Bibliography

Books and articles

Anon.
    1955   *A Picture Book*, BMA (Baltimore Museum of Art?).

Abul Fazl 'Allami
    1835   *The Ain I Akbari by Abul Fazl 'Allami*, trans. from the original Persian by H. Blochmann, MA, Calcutta.

Arnold, Sir Thomas W.
    1965   *Painting in Islam – a study of the place of Pictorial Art in Muslim Culture*, with an introduction by B. W. Robinson, New York: Dover Publications.

Beattie, May H.
    1961   'The Burrell Collection of Oriental Rugs', *Oriental Art*, new series VII: 4, pp. 3–10.
    1968   'Seven Centuries of Oriental Rugs', *Oriental Art* XIV: 3, pp. 170–5.
    1972   *The Thyssen-Bornemisza Collection of Oriental Rugs*, Villa Favorita, Castagnola-Ticino.
    1974   'Oriental Rugs in the Metropolitan Museum of Art', review article, *Oriental Art* XX: 4, pp. 449–52.

Berberyan, Ohan Stepan and Thomson, W. G.
    1924   *A Catalogue of Carpets of Spain and the Orient in the Collection of Charles Deering, Esq.*, London.

Bernheimer, Otto
    1959   *Alte Teppiche des 16. bis 18. Jahrhunderts der Firma L. Bernheimer*, Munich.

von Bode, Wilhelm and Kühnel, Ernst
    1922   *Vorderasiatische Knüpfteppiche aus Älterer Zeit*, Leipzig.
    1955   *Vorderasiatische Knüpfteppiche aus Alter Zeit*, Brunswick.
    1958   *Antique Rugs from the Near East*, 4th rev. ed., trans. by Charles Grant Ellis, Brunswick, Berlin.

Cammann, Schuyler van R.
    1972   'Symbolic Meanings in Oriental Rug Patterns: Parts I, II, III', *Textile Museum Journal*, December, pp. 5–54.
    1974   'Cosmic Symbolism on Carpets from the Sanguszko Group', in *Studies in Art and Literature of the Near East*, pp. 181–208, Peter Chelkowski (ed.), New York.
    1975   'The Systematic Study of Oriental Rugs: Techniques and Patterns', *Journal of the American Oriental Society* 85:2, April-June, pp. 248–60.

Chardin, Sir John
    1735   *Voyages du Chevalier Chardin en Perse*, 4 vols., Amsterdam.

Clarke, C. Purdon (ed.)
    1892   *Oriental Carpets*, Vienna.

Conway, Sir W. Martin
    1913   'A Persian Garden Carpet', *Burlington Magazine* XXIII: 95f.

D'Allemagne, Henry-René
    1911   *Du Khorassan au Pays des Backhtiaris – Trois mois de voyage en Perse*, Paris.

Dilley, A. U.
    1959   *Oriental Rugs and Carpets*, rev. ed., New York.
Dimand, M. S.
    1935   *A Guide to an Exhibition of Oriental Rugs and Textiles*, New York.
    1940   'A Persian Garden Carpet in the Jaipur Museum', *Ars Islamica* VII, pp. 93–6.
Dimand, M. S./Mailey, Jean
    1973   *Oriental Rugs in the Metropolitan Museum of Art*, New York.
Ellis, Charles Grant
    1962   'Gifts from Kashan to Cairo', *Textile Museum Journal* I: 1, November, pp. 33–46.
    1964   'The Little Gems of Ardabil', *Textile Museum Journal* I:3, December, pp. 18–20.
    1965   'Some Compartment Designs for Carpets, and Herat, *Textile Museum Journal* I:4, December, pp. 42–56.
    1968   'Kirman's Heritage in Washington: Vase Rugs in the Textile Museum', *Textile Museum Journal* II: 3, December, pp. 17–34.
    1970   'Caucasian Carpets in the Textile Museum', *Forschungen zür Kunst Asiens – In Memoriam Kurt Erdmann*, pp. 195–208, Istanbul.
Erdmann, Kurt
    1931   'Il Tappeto con Figure d'Animali nel Museo Bardini a Firenze', *Dedalo* XI: 647–63.
    1932a   'Tappeti Persiani', *Dedalo* XII: 707–38.
    1932b   'Persische Wirkteppiche der Safidenzeit', *Pantheon* V: 227–31.
    1938   'Ein persischer Wirkteppich der Safawidenzeit', *Pantheon* XI: 62–6.
    1941   'The Art of Carpet Making' in a Survey of Persian Art, Rezension, *Ars Islamica*, VIII: 121–91.
    1942   'Orientteppiche in deutschen Museen', *Zeitschrift der Deutschen Morgenländischen Gesellschaft*, Bd. 96 (Neue Folge Band 21), pp. 393–417, Leipzig.
    1943   'Teppicherwerbungen der Islamischen Abteilung', *Berliner Museen*, Berichte aus den Preussischen Kunstsammlungen. LXIV: Heft 1–2, pp. 5–17.
    1953   'Die Ausstellung "Orientalische Teppiche aus 4 Jahrhunderten" in Hamburg' (Eine Selbstrezension), OLZ (Orientalische Literatur Zeitung), XLVIII: 5/6, cols 197–205.
    1957   'Arazzi e Tappeti Antiche. Von Mercedes Viale und Vittorio Viale' (review article), *Ars Orientalis* II: 571–89.
    1960   *Oriental Carpets – An Account of their History*, trans. by Charles Grant Ellis, London.
    1961   'Ein Persischer Teppich im Museum für Kunst und Gewerbe', *Jahrbuch der Hamburger Kunstsammlungen* 6: 149–58.
    1962a   'Teppicherwerbungen der Islamischen Abteilung 1956–1961', *Berliner Museen* XII: NF XII: 40–9.
    1962b   'Garten Teppiche', *Heimtex* XIV: 9, pp. 37–40. *Berliner Museen* XII: NF XII: 40–9.
    1970   *Seven Hundred Years of Oriental Carpets*, trans. by May H. Beattie and Hildegard Herzog, London.
Ettinghausen, Richard
    1940   '"Six Thousand Years of Persian Art", The exhibition of Iranian Art, New York', *Ars Islamica* VII: 108–10 (carpet section).
    1971   'The Boston Hunting Carpet in Historical Perspective', *Boston Museum Bulletin* LXIX: 355 and 356, pp. 70–81.
    1972   *Persian Art – Calouste Gulbenkian Collection*, Lisbon.
Fryer, John
    1912   *A New Account of East India and Persia, being Nine Years' Travels*

1672–1681, ed. with notes and an introduction by William Crooke, BA, 3 vols., Hakluyt Society, Second Series, No. XX, London.

P. Fr. Florencio del Nino Jesus, C. D.
    1930   *Biblioteca Carmelitano-Teresiana de Misiones*, III: *En Persia (1608–1624)*, Pamplona (from Spuhler 1968a, p. 137).

Glück, H. and Diez, E.
    1925   *Die Kunst des Islam*, Berlin.

Gouvea, A. de
    1646   *Relations des grandes Guerres.*

Grote-Hasenbalg, Werner
    1922   *Der Orientteppich, seine Geschichte und seine Kultur*, Berlin.

Heinemann, Rudolf J.
    1958   *Sammlung Schloss Rohoncz*, Villa Favorita, Castagnola-Lugano.

Heinz, Dora
    1956   *Alte Orientteppiche*, Darmstadt.
    1970   'Die persischen Teppiche im Österreichischen Museum für angewandte Kunst', *Österreichische Zeitschrift zür Kultur, Politik und Wirtschaft der Islamischen Länder bustan*, pp. 23–8.

Hoare, Oliver
    1971   'Buying old Rugs for less than £100', *The Antique Collectors Club*, 5: 9, January, pp. 10–13.

Ipsiroglu, M. S.
    1967   *Painting and Culture of the Mongols*, trans. from the German with an introduction by E. D. Phillips, London.

Irwin, John
    1955   *Shawls*, Victoria and Albert Museum, London.

Jacoby, Heinrich
    1923   *Eine Sammlung orientalischer Teppiche*, Berlin.
    1952   *How to know Oriental Carpets and Rugs*, ed. by R. J. La Fontaine, London.

Jettmar, Karl
    1967   *Art of the Steppes*, trans. by Ann E. Keep, New York.

Kaempfer, Engelbert
    1684   *Amoenitatum exoticarum politico-physico-medicarum fasciculi V etc.* See Spuhler, 1968a, p. 141.

Kendrick, A. F.
    1914   *Guide to an Exhibition of Tapestries, Carpets and Furniture Lent by The Earl of Dalkeith*, March–May (V&A Museum Pub. No. 95T).
    1929   'Garden Designs in Oriental Carpets', *International Studio*, October, pp. 25–8.

Kendrick, A. F. and Tattersall, C. E. C.
    1973   *Hand-woven Carpets, Oriental and European*, New York: Dover Publications (London 1922).

Kodama, Y. et al. (eds)
    1962   *Illustrated Outline of the Cultural History of Japan*, VIII: *The Azuchi-Monoyama Period*, reprint (first pub. Tokyo 1956, in Japanese).

Kühnel, Ernst
    1930   'Die Orientteppiche der Sammlung Alfred Cassirer', *Kunst und Kunstler* XXVIII: 461–5.
    1957   'Ein neuerworbener Persischer Tierteppich', *Berliner Museen* Berichte aus den ehemaligen Preussischen Kunstsammlungen N.F., VII: 5–11.

Lanier, Mildred B.
    1975   *English and Oriental Carpets at Williamsburg*, Williamsburg.

W.G.M.
 1931　'Persian and other Carpets and Rugs of the Sixteenth to the Eighteenth century at the Jekyll Galleries, 74 South Audley Street, London W1', *Apollo* 13, January–June, p. 139f.

Mańkowski, Tadeusz
 1937　'On Persian Rugs of the so-called Polish type', *Ars Islamica* IV: 456–9.
 1939　'Some Documents from Polish Sources relating to Carpet Making in the time of Shah 'Abbas I', *Survey of Persian Art*, pp. 2431–6.

Martin, F. R.
 1908　*A History of Oriental Carpets before 1800*, Vienna.

Marye, G.
 1894　'L'Exposition d'Art Musulman', *Gazette des Beaux Arts* XI: Carpets, p. 70f.

McMullan, Joseph V.
 1965　*Islamic Carpets*, New York.

Migeon, Gaston
 1903a　'L'Exposition des Arts Musulmans au Musée des Arts Décoratifs', *Les Arts* XIII: 2–34.
 1903b　*Exposition des Arts Musulmans au Musée des Arts Décoratifs* (100 plates), Paris.
 1909　*La Collection Kelekian. Étoffes & Tapis d'Orient & de Venise*, Paris.
 1922　*Musée du Louvre. L'Orient Musulman*, Paris.
 1927　*Manuel d'Art Musulman – Arts Plastiques et Industriels*, 2 vols., Paris.

Mumford, John Kimberley
 1940　*The Yerkes Collection of Rugs and Carpets* fully described by J. K. Mumford, New York, Leipzig, London, Toronto.

Orendi, Julius
 1930　*Das Gesamtwissen über antike und neue Teppiche des Orients*, 2 vols., Vienna.

Oettingen, R. von and Grote-Hasenbalg, Werner
 1921　*Meisterstücke orientalischer Knüpfkunst*, Neubearbeitet nach R. v. Oettingen und erweitert von Werner Grote-Hasenbalg. Mappe I, II, Vienna.

Ovington, J.
 1696　*A Voyage to Suratt in the Year 1689 by J. Ovington, M.A. Chaplain to His Majesty*, London.

Pinder-Wilson, Ralph
 1957　*Islamic Art – One Hundred Plates in Colour with an Introductory Essay on Islamic Art*, London.

Pope, Arthur Upham
 1923　'Oriental Rugs as Fine Art, III: Persian Carpets of the XVI Century', *International Studio* LXXVI: 322–32.

Pope, Arthur Upham and Ackerman, Phyllis
 1939　*A Survey of Persian Art*, vols. III and VIII, edition de luxe, London.

Riefstahl, R. M.
 1925　'Turkish "Bird" Rugs and Their Design', *The Art Bulletin* VII: 91–5.

Robinson, Gertrude
 1938　'An Unknown Sixteenth-Century Persian Carpet', *Burlington Magazine* 72: 1, pp. 102–5.

Rudenko, Sergei I.
 1970　*Frozen Tombs of Siberia – the Pazyryk Burials of Iron Age Horsemen*, trans. and with a preface by M. W. Thompson.

Sarre, Friedrich
 1903 'Die Ausstellung muhammedanischer Kunst in Paris', *Repertorium für Kunstwissenschaft* XXVI: 521–35.
 1910 'Die Teppiche auf der Mohammedanischen Ausstellung in München 1910', *Kunst und Kunsthandwerk* XIII: 469–86.
 1921 'Ein Neuerworbener Gartenteppich', *Berliner Museen* XLII: 54–9.
Sarre, F. and Martin, F. R.
 1912 *Die Ausstellung von Meisterwerken Muhammedanischer Kunst in München 1910, Die Teppiche*, supp. vol. IV Photographische Original-Aufnahmen München.
Sarre, Friedrich and Trenkwald, Hermann
 1926–9 *Old Oriental Carpets*, trans. by A. F. Kendrick, 2 vols., Vienna and Leipzig.
Scala, A. von, Bode, Wilhelm, Sarre, Friedrich
 1908 *Altorientalische Teppiche*, Leipzig.
Schlosser, Ignaz
 1963 *European and Oriental Rugs and Carpets*, London.
Schürmann, Ulrich
 1966 *Oriental Carpets*, London.
Spuhler, Friedrich
 1964 'Eine Ausstellung orientalischer Teppiche in Temple Newsam House, Leeds', *Weltkunst* XXXIV: 15, pp. 593–4.
 1968a *Seidene Repräsentationsteppiche der mittleren bis späten Safawidenzeit. Die sog. Polenteppiche*, Inaugural Dissertation, Berlin.
 1968b Joseph V. McMullan, 'Islamic Carpets', review, *Kunst des Orients* V: 1, pp. 62–6.
 1970 'Zur Ausstellung "Islamische Teppiche" der Sammlung Joseph V. McMullans in Frankfurt-am-Main', *Pantheon* XXVIII: 2, p. 141f.
Stead, Rexford
 1974 *The Ardabil Carpets*, The J. Paul Getty Museum. Malibu, California.
Tattersall, Creassey (C.E.C.)
 1931 'Carpets and Textiles at the Persian Exhibition', *Apollo* XIII: January–June, pp. 1–9.
 1934 *A History of British Carpets: From the Introduction of the Craft until the Present Day*, London.
Tavernier, Johann Baptiste
 1676 *Les Six Voyages de J. B. Tavernier en Tarquie en Perse et aux Indes*, Paris.
Teixeira, Pedro
 1902 *The Travels of Pedro Teixeira*; with his 'Kings of Harmuz' and Extracts from his 'Kings of Persia', trans. and annotated by William F. Sinclair, Bombay Civil Service (Retd.); with further notes and an introduction by Donald Ferguson. Hakluyt Society, Second Series No. IX.
Troll, Siegfried
 1951 *Altorientalische Teppiche*, Vienna.
Wace, A. G. B.
 1931 'Persische Stickereien auf der Ausstellung im Burlington House', *Pantheon* VII: 211–15.
Wiet, Gaston
 1932 'L'Exposition d'Art Persan à Londres', *Syria* XIII: 96.
 1933 *L'Exposition persane de 1931*, Cairo.
 1935 *L'Exposition d'Art Persan*, 2 vols, Cairo.

Exhibition catalogues and guides

Berlin
Museum für Islamische Kunst
    1971   Brisch, K. et al, *Museum für Islamische Kunst Berlin.*
Schloss Charlottenburg (Langhansbau)
    n.d.   *Islamische Kunst,* Ausstellung des Museums für Islamische Kunst.

Cambridge, Mass.
Fogg Art Museum
    1949   *Rugs of Turkey, Persia and Central Asia from the Collection of Joseph V. McMullan,* 11 March–23 April (mimeo. cat.).
    1974   Welch, Anthony, *Shah 'Abbas & the Arts of Isfahan,* 19 January–24 February (see New York, Asia House Gallery).

Chicago
Art Club of Chicago
    1926   Pope, Arthur Upham, *Early Oriental Carpets,* January.
Art Institute
    1947   Kelley, Charles Fabens, and Gentles, Margaret O., *An Exhibition of Antique Oriental Rugs,* 6 February–16 March.

Frankfurt
Museum für Kunsthandwerk
    1968–9   Schürmann, Ulrich, *Islamische Teppiche – The Joseph V. McMullan Collection New York,* 7 December–January.
    1971–2   *Persische Teppiche,* 19 November–January (see Hamburg).

Glasgow
Glasgow Art Gallery and Museum, Kelvingrove
    1969   *Carpets and Tapestries from the Burrell Collection,* 23 June–16 August.
McLellan Galleries
    1949   *The Burrell Collection.*
    1951   *The Burrell Collection.*

Hamburg
Museum für Kunst und Gewerbe
    1950   Erdmann, Kurt, *Orientalische Teppiche aus vier Jahrhunderten,* 22 August–22 October.
    1971   *Persische Teppiche,* 24 September–7 November.

Kendal
Abbot Hall Art Gallery
    1967   *1000 Years of Persian Art,* 28 September–5 November (section on 'Persian Miniature Painting' by B. W. Robinson).

Leeds
Temple Newsam House
    1964   Beattie, May H., *The Rug in Islamic Art,* 16 April–28 May.

London
Hayward Gallery
    1972   *Islamic Carpets from the Joseph V. McMullan Collection,* 19 October–10 December, Arts Council of Great Britain.
    1975   *Treasures from the Burrell Collection,* 18 March–4 May, Arts Council of Great Britain.

Royal Academy of Arts
  1931   *Catalogue of the International Exhibition of Persian Art at the Royal Academy of Arts*, 7 January–28 February.

Victoria and Albert Museum
  1914   Kendrick, A. F., *Guide to an Exhibition of Tapestries, Carpets and Furniture Lent by The Earl of Dalkeith,* March–May (V&A Museum Pub. No. 95T).
  1920   Kendrick, A. F., *Guide to the Collection of Carpets*, 2nd ed., Dept. of Textiles.

Munich
  1910   *Amt. Katalog von Meisterwerken Muhammadanischer Kunst I.*
Museum für Völkerkunde
  1963   *Persische Kunst*, Katalog zür Ausstellung des Staatlichen Museums für Völkerkunde.
Neue Pinakothek
  1930   *Sammlung Schloss Rohoncz. II Plastik und Kunstgewerbe.*

New York
Altman & Co.
  1923   *A Collection of Antique Carpets.*
Asia House Gallery
  1973   Welch, Anthony, *Shah ʿAbbas & the Arts of Isfahan*, 11 October–2 December.
Iranian Institute
  1940   Ackermann, P., *Guide to the exhibition of Persian Art.*
Metropolitan Museum of Art
  1923   Breck, Joseph and Morris, Frances, *The James F. Ballard Collection of Oriental Rugs*, October.
  1930   Dimand, M. S., *Loan Exhibition of Persian Rugs of the so-called Polish Type*, 10 June–21 September
  1935   Dimand, M. S., *A Guide to an Exhibition of Oriental Rugs and Textiles*, 13 May–15 September.

Paris
Musée des Arts Décoratifs
  1903   Migeon, G., van Berchem, Huant, M. H., *Catalogue descriptif – Exposition des Arts Musulmans.*
Orangerie des Tuileries
  1971   *Arts de l'Islam – des origines à 1700 dans les collections publiques françaises*, 22 June–30 August.

San Francisco
M. H. de Young Memorial Museum
  1937   Aga Oglu, Mehmet (carpet section), *Exhibition of Islamic Art*, 24 February–22 May.

Washington
Textile Museum
  1948   Anon (Aga Oglu), *Dragon Rugs. A loan exhibition from American public and private collections*, 18 October–19 November.
  1965–6 J. V. M., *Rugs from the Joseph V. McMullan Collection*, November–January.
  1967   *Textile Museum Sampler.*
  1969   Landreau, Anthony N. and Pickering, W. R., *From the Bosporus to Samarkand: Flat-Woven Rugs*, 25 May–27 September.

1972   Ettinghausen, Richard, *From Persia's Ancient Looms*, 23 January–30 September.

1975–6 Ellis, Charles Grant, *Early Caucasian Rugs, Textile Museum 50th Anniversary 1925–74*, 11 November–6 March.

Zurich
Kunstgewerbemuseum

1936   Sarre, Friedrich and Sautier, Albert, *Ausstellung Iranische Kunst, Elamitischer und persischer kulturkreis*, 19 May–19 July.

Kunsthaus

1962   *Kunstschätze aus Iran von der Prähistorischen bis zür Islamischen Zeit*, 2nd ed., 27 May–5 August (introduction R. Wehrli).

Sale catalogues

London
Sotheby & Co.

1972   *Good English Furniture . . . Fine Rugs and Carpets etc.*, Friday 30 June.

Milan
Rizzoli & C.

1934   XIII *Vendita all'Asta di una collezione de antici Tappeti Classici Orientali de signor Alby Ghernon etc.*

New York
American Art Association, Inc.

1925   *The V. & L. Benguiat Private Collection of Rare Old Rugs*, 4 and 5 December.

1927   *The Alphonse Kann Collection*, 6–8 January.